A Season to Forget

A Season to Forget

THE STORY OF THE 1988
BALTIMORE ORIOLES

RON SNYDER

**SPORTS
PUBLISHING**

Sports Publishing books may be purchased in bulk at special discounts for sales promotion, corporate gifts, fund-raising, or educational purposes. Special editions can also be created to specifications. For details, contact the Special Sales Department, Sports Publishing, 307 West 36th Street, 11th Floor, New York, NY 10018 or sportspubbooks@skyhorsepublishing.com.

Sports Publishing® is a registered trademark of Skyhorse Publishing, Inc.®, a Delaware corporation.

Visit our website at www.sportspubbooks.com.

10 9 8 7 6 5 4 3 2 1

Library of Congress Cataloging-in-Publication Data is available on file.

Cover design by Qualcom
Cover photo courtesy of the Baltimore Orioles

Print ISBN: 978-1-68358-262-5
Ebook ISBN: 978-1-68358-263-2

Printed in the United States of America

To my wife, Lori, and my children, William, Marissa, and Megan. Thank you for always being there for me, supporting me and motivating me to be a better husband, father, and person each day.

To my parents, brother, in-laws, and my entire extended family, thank you for having faith in me, being there for my family and offering me words of encouragement when needed.

CONTENTS

CONTENTS

AUTHOR'S NOTE

Press boxes across the country—from the smallest community colleges to the largest NFL, NBA, and MLB stadium, and arenas—are filled with talented sports journalists filing stories and relaying news of the teams they are covering.

There is an unwritten rule that there is no cheering in the press box. Reporters, justly so, are supposed to be objective observers who show no biases in the teams and games they cover. Such an approach leads to quality game recaps, feature stories, notebooks, and social media posts so that those who follow the teams can be informed on how they performed both on and off the field.

The unspoken mantra in the press box is while the newspaper reporters, columnists, sportscasters, talk show hosts, podcasters, and bloggers remain professional on the job, they likely got into this profession because they were, first and foremost, fans of the game. They likely dreamt of the day they would be paid to be front and center getting to watch and report on the favorite teams of their childhood in the Super Bowl, World Series, Stanley Cup, etc.

I was no different from any of those aspiring journalists. When I realized I was never going to be the next Larry Bird, playing small forward for the Boston Celtics, I thought the next best thing would be to cover the team for the *Boston Globe*.

While many children my age ran downstairs on Sunday mornings to catch the latest highlights from the previous night's games on *SportsCenter*, I was more interested in waiting for the "Sports Reporters" to come on TV. I envisioned myself one day sitting next to the likes of Bob Ryan, Mike Lupica, Mitch Albom, Dick Schaap, and Michael Wilbon, opining on the latest sports news and controversies of the day. I never quite made it to the *Globe* or ESPN, but I have been blessed to cover my hometown teams in Maryland and experience more than most who set out in this profession.

From reporting on the Army-Navy football game to watching the Ravens advance to the AFC Championship to covering Johns Hopkins men's lacrosse on its run toward an NCAA title, to following the rise of the University of Maryland women's basketball team under coach Brenda Frese, I have had the chance to be front and center for some of the biggest sports stories in Maryland over the past twenty years.

But to me, none of that was more exciting than getting to be in the press box covering the Baltimore Orioles when they advanced to the American League Championship Series against the Kansas City Royals in 2014. The Orioles were the American League East champions, having posted a record of 96–66, which was 12 games better than the second-place (and dreaded) New York Yankees.

The divisional title would be the Orioles' first since 1997 and came two years after the team snapped a streak of fourteen straight losing seasons. The Orioles' fan base turned out in force to support a franchise which has a history and tradition as strong as just about any team in professional sports.

Even though the Orioles were swept by the Royals in that series, it was great to be covering a relevant baseball team again. That season reminded me of why I wanted to be a sports reporter in the first place. Unfortunately, as good as the Orioles were from 1966 to 1983, when they appeared in six World Series (winning three), they have been largely inconsistent in my lifetime.

This was especially the case during the formative years of my youth. I was just five years old when the Orioles last won a World Series and have no memories of them winning that championship. My first memories of the Orioles came in 1986 and 1987, when the team was in a state of decline.

The first Opening Day I can truly remember was in 1988. I remember going over the roster in the newspaper and trying to figure out whether a team with future Hall of Famers like Cal Ripken Jr. and Eddie Murray and veteran pitchers like Mike Boddicker and Scott McGregor could bounce back and get the Orioles back into contention. If just a few things went right, I thought at the time, my Orioles could surprise their critics.

Then Opening Day arrived and spring was in the air when the Orioles hosted the Milwaukee Brewers in front of a sellout crowd at old Memorial Stadium on 33rd Street in Baltimore. Unfortunately, that feeling of optimism switched into a sense of despair as the Orioles were routed 12–0.

Still, with 161 games to go, my then-nine-year-old self believed my beloved Orioles would come back the next day and get back on the winning track. The Orioles then lost again . . . and again . . . and again. The team then fired their manager six games into the season, yet they kept losing.

Most fans quickly became dismayed at a lost season. Not me. I would watch every game I could that aired on TV. And on the other nights I would listen to Jon Miller and Joe Angel's call on my small portable radio tucked under my pillow and the volume low enough so my parents wouldn't know I was still awake.

Each night for twenty-one games I was disappointed, and each night I would repeat the same drill hoping they would finally get a win. Then on April 29, 1988, the Orioles finally won, and I ran around the house screaming and jumping for joy that the record-setting losing streak was over. Even at such a young age, I knew the Orioles were destined for a last-place finish, but I did not care. On that night, for that one moment, my team was a winner.

It was those memories and emotions that provided me with the motivation to write *A Season to Forget: The Story of the 1988 Baltimore Orioles*. This book combines my two sports lives: that of the fan and of the reporter. I took an objective look at how the Orioles fell so far and so fast over a five-year period. At the same time, I tried to tap into the enthusiasm of my nine-year-old self and use it to tell a story that every baseball fan of my generation vividly remembers. It is also a story fans today should read to offer perspective that when you think it can't get worse for your team, you only need to remember it's not as bad as it was for the 1988 Baltimore Orioles . . . that is, unless you watched the 2018 Orioles lose a franchise-worst 115 games. At least that team actually *won* on Opening Day.

PREFACE

When Baltimore Orioles shortstop Cal Ripken Jr. caught a line drive off the bat of Philadelphia Phillies center fielder Garry Maddox in the bottom of the ninth of Game Five of the 1983 World Series, it was significant for many reasons.

The out clinched the Orioles' third world championship. It would also cap an amazing seventeen-year run by the organization, who were considered at the time to be one of the premier franchises in all of professional sports. That catch by Ripken would also be the last World Series moment the Orioles would experience for thirty-five years (and counting). The franchise would soon experience a precipitous slide that would affect the team for years to come.

Between 1966 and 1983, the Baltimore Orioles were considered the best team in baseball. During that span, they won three World Series, advanced to three others, and competed for a playoff spot in just about every season.

The Orioles were a model franchise thanks to their "Orioles Way" approach of building from the ground up, starting with their farm system. Future Hall of Famers like third baseman Brooks Robinson, pitcher Jim Palmer, shortstop/third baseman Cal Ripken Jr., and first baseman Eddie Murray made their way through the ranks and helped put consistent winners on the field.

But five years after Ripken caught the final out to clinch the '83 World Series, the franchise was in a state of disarray. From not understanding how to utilize free agency to having their once-famed farm system dry up of quality talent and failed trades, a once-proud franchise was in a downward spiral.

Heading into the 1988 season, the Orioles expected to struggle after a 95-loss season the year before and sub-par seasons the two previous years. Not even the return of famed manager Earl Weaver in 1985 and 1986 was enough to correct the Orioles' path. The franchise attempted to revamp their roster in 1988 by bringing in fourteen new players.

While not expecting to compete for a playoff spot, not even the most knowledgeable baseball experts thought the Orioles were going to be historically bad. They were wrong. Baltimore opened that season with a record of 0–21, shattering the record for futility to start a season by eight games.

From a 12–0 Opening Day loss to the Milwaukee Brewers in front of a then-franchise-record 52,395 fans at old Memorial Stadium to a 4–2 loss against the Minnesota Twins at the Hubert H Humphrey Metrodome, the Orioles found different ways to lose each night. It got so bad that even President Ronald Reagan sent a message of support to the loveable losers from Charm City. Religious leaders, psychics, and mental health professionals even offered to help the team find a path to that elusive first win.

By the time they finally won a game—a 9–0 victory against the Chicago White Sox at old Comiskey Park on April 29, 1988—the damage was already done. The Orioles were already 15 1/2 games out of first place in the American League East before May 1. They went on to finish the season with a 54–107 record, 34 1/2 games out of first and 23 1/2 games behind the next worst team in the division (the 78–84 Cleveland Indians).

The high point of the season came on the Orioles' next home game after their first win when an announced crowd of 50,402 came out to support the team on "Fantastic Fans Night." That was also the date that then-Maryland Governor William Donald Schaeffer announced a fifteen-year lease agreement between the Orioles and the Maryland Stadium Authority to house the team in a new stadium in downtown Baltimore (which would eventually become Oriole Park at Camden Yards).

But the question remains: How did a once model franchise like the Baltimore Orioles devolve into a team with the distinction of having the worst start of any team in MLB history?

INTRODUCTION

To understand how the Orioles reached the nadir of professional sports just five years after winning a world championship, one must first look back at the course the franchise traveled. The roots of the team date back to 1901, when they were known as the Milwaukee Brewers, one of eight original teams in the American League. The franchise then moved to St. Louis and was renamed the Browns in 1902, where they spent fifty-two years before relocating to Baltimore in 1954.

The seeds for the Orioles' greatest success were planted when the team hired Paul Richards in September 1954 as the team's manager and general manager. It was at this time that the "Orioles Way" was developed. The philosophy, which has gained iconic status among baseball lore, became the blueprint for success.

The Orioles Way stressed uniform baseball fundamentals at every level of the organization. Players would only advance through the system when they were absolutely ready to do so, ensuring top prospects were not rushed along too quickly to the next level. The combination of instruction, scouting, and player development laid the foundation for years of success.

A uniform philosophy was just one aspect of the Orioles' success. The organization was also blessed with knowledgeable baseball personnel from top to bottom. Richards is credited with stocking the team with pitchers like Milt Papas and Dave McNally, as well as future All-Star and American League MVP Boog Powell and future Hall of Fame third baseman Brooks Robinson.

"We just had a great ability to develop players during that time period," said Robinson, an 18-time All-Star who played for the Orioles from 1955 to 1977 and was inducted into the National Baseball Hall of Fame in 1983. "We were so deep there were players who stayed in the minors longer than they would have otherwise with other teams because there were just no spaces for them with the big-league ballclub."

Lee MacPhail added another layer to the Oriole Way when he became general manager in 1958. It was at that time that MacPhail established cross-checkers in the scouting department to ensure the team was making sound decisions before offering contracts to potential prospects.

The Orioles slowly began to develop into a championship contender in the early- to mid-1960s thanks to a deep roster and farm system. However, the team came up just short of making the playoffs in 1965.[1] This led the organization to make a move which would end up putting them over the top. Prior to the following season, new

---

1   During this time the top team from each league (AL and NL) would face off in the World Series. Despite winning 94 games in 1965, the Orioles finished in third place behind the Chicago White Sox (95) and Minnesota Twins (102).

general manager Harry Dalton—who was previously successful as the team's farm director—pulled the trigger on a deal that would land Baltimore future Hall of Fame outfielder Frank Robinson in exchange for pitchers Milt Pappas and Jack Baldschun, and outfielder Dick Simpson.

The trade is considered one of the most lopsided in the history of professional baseball. In his first season in Baltimore, Robinson batted .316, hit 49 home runs, and drove in 122 runs en route to capturing the American League MVP and leading the Orioles to their first World Series championship.[2] The team captured the World Series with a four-game sweep of the Los Angeles Dodgers (where Robinson was also named Series MVP).

The Orioles, who also hired future Hall of Fame manager Earl Weaver in 1968, would go on to advance to the World Series three more times during Robinson's six years with the team. Baltimore won it all in 1970 over Robinson's former team, the Cincinnati Reds, while being upset in 1969 and 1971 by the New York Mets and Pittsburgh Pirates, respectively.

Throughout the 1970s, the Orioles would remain competitive thanks again to a strong minor-league system and the ability to make several key trades. They would go on to win the AL East title in 1973 and 1974 but were eliminated each year by the Oakland A's in the American League Championship Series. These steps would help pave the way for their 1983 World Series title, making it three wins in six Series appearances over a 17-year period.

The development of young players, like second baseman Bobby Grich and third baseman Doug DeCinces, allowed the team to trade

---

2   Frank Robinson is the first and only player to ever win MVP awards in both leagues, winning the award in 1961 as a member of the Reds.

longtime second baseman Davey Johnson after the 1972 season, which gave them an heir apparent to third baseman Brooks Robinson, who retired in 1977.

Baltimore native and long-time sports reporter Jeff Seidel said that the Orioles had an embarrassment of riches during this era and were an organization that was the envy of much of baseball—if not all of sports. "In the end, that depth was what made the Orioles confident to trade Davey Johnson [following the 1972 season] to pave the way for Bobby Grich at second base, and trade Frank Robinson to make room for Al Bumbry around the same time."

DeCinces, who spent eight seasons of his 15-year career with the Orioles, went on to hit one of the most famous home runs in team history on June 22, 1979. It was that date when he connected on a two-run home run with two outs in the bottom of the ninth off Detroit Tigers pitcher Dave Tobik to give the Orioles a 6–5 victory at Memorial Stadium in Baltimore. The win has been recognized as the night "Oriole Magic" was born. The Orioles went on to advance to the World Series before losing to the Pirates in a classic seven-game series (despite jumping out to a three-games-to-one lead).

The 1979 Orioles, who won 102 games, also included home-grown pitchers Mike Flanagan, as well as future Hall of Fame pitcher Jim Palmer and first baseman Eddie Murray. In addition, other key contributors included catcher Rick Dempsey, starting pitcher Scott McGregor, and relief pitcher/closer Tippy Martinez. Those three players, along with pitchers Dave Pagan and Rudy May, were acquired by the Orioles on June 15, 1976, from the New York Yankees in exchange for catcher Elrod Hendricks and pitchers Doyle Alexander, Ken Holtzman, Grant Jackson, and Jimmy Freeman. Many consider that another lopsided trade in the Orioles' favor, which was orchestrated by then-general manager Hank Peters in his first year at the helm after Frank Cashen, who served as general manager from 1971 to 1978, stepped down from the position.

Flanagan, Palmer, Murray, Dempsey, McGregor, and Martinez, along with draft picks like pitcher Mike Boddicker and Cal Ripken Jr. provided much of the core for the buildup to the team's 1983 championship squad. Ripken, who was in just his second full season in 1983, finished the year batting .318 with 27 home runs, 102 RBIs, 211 hits, and 121 runs scored on his way to the first of his nineteen All-Star appearances and the first of his two MVP awards.

Dempsey, who spent twelve seasons of his 23-year career with the Orioles, was named World Series MVP after he batted .385 with a .923 slugging percentage against the Phillies. With a core of Ripken Jr. and Murray in the lineup and pitchers like Flanagan, Boddicker, McGregor, and Storm Davis at or near their prime, the organization and their fans believed the 1983 title would just be the latest of many to follow in Baltimore. However, a combination of poor drafting, questionable free agent signings, and other personnel decisions would lead to a quick decline for a franchise with a rich and proud tradition.

Ripken, who entered the National Baseball Hall of Fame in 2007, said the seeds for the 1983 Orioles were planted during the 1982 campaign when Baltimore missed out on the AL East title and, just as importantly, a playoff spot in the final game of the season against the Milwaukee Brewers. That year, the Orioles struggled for much of the first half of the season and were under .500 as late as June 6 before rallying. The surge began on August 20, as they reeled off seven straight victories. After losing the second game of a doubleheader on August 27, they began a 10-game winning streak the following night, cutting an eight-game deficit to just two games by September 7.

The Orioles entered the final week of the '82 season trailing the Brewers by three games but would be facing them in a four-game series at home. The Orioles won the first three games of the series by a combined score of 26–7, setting the stage for a winner-take-all contest on October 3, 1982.

Unfortunately for Baltimore fans, the Brewers jumped out to a 3–0 lead after three innings and broke the game open with five runs in the ninth to give them a 10–2 victory. Despite the loss, the sellout crowd stood and cheered for 45 minutes to honor Weaver, who announced earlier in the year that he would be retiring after the season.

"Growing up in and around the team, you got to know and expect winning and being around a championship caliber team," said Ripken, who began his record-setting consecutive games played streak on May 30, 1982. "I wasn't sure what to expect in 1982. We got off to such a slow start and then came on like gangbusters in the end and rallied all the way back to tie the Brewers heading into that final game of the season. We had Jim Palmer going on the mound and he had won like eleven decisions in a row at one point that season, but we came up short in the end.[3]

"As we watched Milwaukee celebrate after that game, it made all of us think about where we could have made up that game over the course of the season," Ripken continued. "That really helped us focus and get prepared for the 1983 season. Of course, it all came together for us that season and we went on to win the division fairly easily and won the World Series. I really thought there would be more in our future."

Sportscaster Roy Firestone can attest to just how great the Orioles were during the franchise's golden age. In addition to reporting on many of those great teams and players, Firestone is an unabashed

---

3   Palmer won 11 straight decisions from June 7 to September 4, with seven no-decisions (though the Orioles would win four).

lifelong Oriole fan. Firestone, who was sixty-four at the time of this book's publication, grew up in Miami Beach, Florida, and served as a spring training batboy for the team for several seasons as a teenager in the 1960s. The relationships he built during that time would come full circle when he spoke at the unveiling of a statue honoring Brooks Robinson at Oriole Park at Camden Yards in 2012.

"When I was growing up, the Orioles were one of, if not the best franchise in all of baseball from 1964 to 1983," said Firestone, who hosted ESPN's interview program *Up Close* from 1980 to 1994. "The team was so stacked with players, there were many stuck in the minors because they could not earn a spot among those ahead of them. That was the case for players like Don Baylor or Bobby Grich, who only got a spot because the Orioles finally traded Davey Johnson.

"The Orioles were just an amazing model franchise in every sense of the word. From the players on the field, to the managers and coaches, to the executives to the scouting to the player development staff," Firestone continued. "In many ways, the front office was just like the players in that some really talented people had to leave to get a shot because of the people entrenched in front of them."

Baltimore attorney and sports agent Ron Shapiro agrees. Shapiro understands the business of sports as well as anyone. Many have dubbed the Shapiro family "The First Family of Sports Management." Ron Shapiro's son Mark entered 2019 as the president and CEO of the Toronto Blue Jays, a role he began in August 2015. This came after he spent twenty-four seasons with the Cleveland Indians, where he began in player development and eventually rose through the ranks to become general manager. Coincidentally, he was recommended for the job by Peters.

In 1983, just about the entire Orioles roster was represented by Ron Shapiro and that World Series team was and still remains a sense of pride for him. Shapiro said after seeing the team come so close to a title in 1979 and 1982, he was ecstatic to see the Orioles go all the way and bring home the championship in 1983.

"The success of the Orioles was very personal to me," said Shapiro. "It was extraordinary to watch the team win the World Series in 1983. That was the culmination of many years of hard work. The team overcame the adversity of losing a heartbreaking World Series to the Pittsburgh Pirates in 1979, and then dealt with the agony of just missing out on the playoffs in 1982. I represented about twenty-one players associated with that roster in 1983, including eighteen or so who were with the team at the start of the World Series.

"My dream as an agent was to achieve the best contractual deal for my clients and find a way for them to remain together and accomplish the goal of winning a championship," Shapiro continued. "That's exactly what happened in 1983. It was really cool to see that come to fruition after so many years of hard work and heartbreak."

Michael Gibbons, a Baltimore sports historian and longtime director emeritus of the Babe Ruth Birthplace Museum, said the Orioles' stretch of success provided a blueprint for any sports franchise who wanted to build a championship-contending team.

"The Orioles just went about it the right way for so long," Gibbons said. "They understood how to develop talent and play baseball following all the fundamentals you are taught from Little League to high school and through the minor leagues. Fans thought the run would keep going. We never thought it would be more than thirty-five years between World Series appearances for the Orioles."

Chapter One

THE LONG, HARD, FAST DECLINE

The Orioles had high hopes for the 1984 season. This was due in large part to the fact that the team returned much of its core roster that won the previous year's World Series. However, their chance at a repeat all but evaporated in the early weeks of the season thanks to AL East rival the Detroit Tigers. The Tigers got off to as strong of a start as any team in recent history when they won their first nine games, and their impressive play would only continue. They had a record of 35–5 after 40 games en route to a wire-to-wire division title and a 4–1 series victory over the San Diego Padres in the World Series.

Despite a fifth-place finish in the division, the Orioles still managed to win 85 games. That year, Boddicker had the best year of his career, going 20–11 with a 2.79 ERA, 128 strikeouts, and 16 complete games. In fact, no Orioles pitcher has won 20 games in a single season since. Cal Ripken Jr. also set an AL record for most assists in a season by a shortstop at 583.

However, the 1984 season was also the end of the road for the great Jim Palmer, who was released after going 0–3 with a 9.17 ERA in a limited role on the mound. The release did little to diminish Palmer's place in baseball history as he finished with a lifetime record of 268–152, with 2,212 strikeouts and three Cy Young awards. A first-ballot Hall of Famer in 1990, Palmer is also the only Oriole player to be a member on all six of the team's World Series rosters.

"I believed we were still really good in 1984, but the Detroit Tigers got off to that amazing 35–5 start, and it was just too difficult for anyone, let alone us, to catch them that year," Ripken Jr. said. "That was a season where we still had the pitching, but our hitting trailed off more than we anticipated it would."

The 1985 season was fairly similar to the previous year's campaign as Baltimore went 83–78 and finished in fourth place in the AL East. The team treaded water all season, which led to some changes in hopes of righting the ship. The Orioles fired manager Joe Altobelli, who was let go after the team started 29–26. Overall, Altobelli posted a record of 212–167 in two-plus seasons at the helm in Baltimore. The Orioles then coaxed Earl Weaver out of retirement and the team went on to win 53 of their remaining 105 games.[1]

While still competitive, it was apparent that the club was in a decline, in part due to injuries to the pitching staff, poor drafting, reaches in free agency and trades that brought in players who were a poor fit for a franchise trying desperately to hold on to past glory. This was on full display in 1985 when the team signed outfielders Fred Lynn and Lee Lacy and reliever/closer Don Aase and traded for second baseman Alan Wiggins.

For those that followed the team—either as fans or media—it was frustrating to see the team struggle to adjust to the changing landscape of Major League Baseball in the 1980s. Observers felt the front

---

1   Cal Ripken Sr. managed one game for the Orioles that season, on June 14, 1985, in which they defeated the Milwaukee Brewers, 8–3.

office and ownership lacked an understanding of free agency and their inability to develop home-grown talent, which took an obvious toll on the franchise.

"Part of the Orioles' struggles began when they took chances on free agency that just did not pan out like they expected," said sportscaster Roy Firestone. "Players like Lee Lacy, Fred Lynn, and Alan Wiggins signed with the team and just were not able to produce like they had with their previous teams. Then, with many of the up-and-coming scouts leaving for other teams, the Orioles just didn't draft and sign players like they had in the past. That takes its toll on the farm system over time."

Lynn was thirty-three years old when he signed as a free agent after spending four seasons with the California Angels. A nine-time All-Star, Lynn was still a bona fide power hitter when he arrived in Baltimore. However, injuries limited him to no more than 124 games in any of his three-plus seasons with the Orioles. He was also not the same fielder that won four Gold Gloves between 1975 and 1980, when he was at his best as a member of the Boston Red Sox.

Lacy was another free agent who had seen better days by the time the Orioles signed the then thirty-seven-year-old. Lacy, who spent the previous six years with the Pittsburgh Pirates, was among the eleven players suspended by Major League Baseball after testifying before a Pittsburgh grand jury that led to a series of drug trials and exposed the cocaine use of many players during that time.

Lacy averaged 112 games a season for the Orioles from 1985 to 1987, with a high of 130 games in 1986. By 1986 he agreed to take drug tests, perform community service, and pay an estimated fine of more than $34,000 rather than be suspended for sixty days for being connected with illegal drugs.

"I'm glad it's behind me," Lacy told reporters on March 2, 1986, regarding the drug issues. "I'm looking forward to helping the Orioles win a pennant. Any time anyone says they're going to take some of your money, it hurts."

Aase signed a four-year, $2.4 million contract with the Orioles in 1985. The 6-foot-3 right hander had experienced decent success in the majors for the Boston Red Sox and California Angels before signing with the Orioles. He was brought in to be the closer with long-time Oriole Tippy Martinez's career winding down.

After an up-and-down year in 1985, which included allowing seven runs in a 12–0 loss against the Red Sox in June, Aase had the best year of his career in 1986. Even though he had a losing record (6–7), he had a 2.98 ERA and 34 saves, which was an Orioles team record at that point. He was selected to the All-Star team and recorded a save after getting San Francisco Giant Chris Brown to hit into a double play in the bottom of the ninth at the old Houston Astrodome. Aase even ended up winning the Orioles MVP award that season.

That season would represent the high point in Aase's career. Injuries would soon take their toll on him not long after the All-Star Game. The first setback was a back injury in August 1986, which occurred while lifting his then-four-year-old son. He then missed most of the 1987 season due to shoulder surgery and was limited to just 35 appearances with a 4.05 ERA and no saves in 1988. In his final two seasons with the Orioles, he pitched just 54 2/3 innings and recorded just two saves in 42 appearances.

Arguably no acquisition was more risky and tragic than that of Wiggins. Originally drafted by the California Angels as the eighth overall pick of the 1977 MLB Amateur Draft out of Pasadena City College, Wiggins would be released about a year later after reportedly being involved in a fight with one of his coaches. He would later sign with the Los Angeles Dodgers before the San Diego Padres selected him in the 1980 Rule 5 Draft.

Despite being one of the better base runners in the game, Wiggins struggled with drug addiction—which included using cocaine, an addiction that was quite prevalent at the time. By 1983, Wiggins was entrenched as the Padres' leadoff hitter in a season when he batted .276 and stole 66 bases, which was good enough for second in the National League.[2] He was even named the team's Most Valuable Player.

By 1984, Wiggins, who moved to second base, became a catalyst in helping the Padres advance to the World Series. That season, he finished second in the National League with 106 runs scored to go along with his 70 stolen bases. The following season should have represented the continuation of a great career for Wiggins, who signed a four-year contract extension worth nearly $3 million. However, it instead represented the beginning of his descent—both professionally and personally.

Wiggins suffered a knee injury during spring training in 1985, which caused him to miss the first five games of the season. He was soon suspended by the Padres following a relapse into cocaine addiction. He followed that by going through a drug rehabilitation program before being traded on June 27, 1985, to the Orioles for pitchers Roy Lee Jackson and Richard Caldwell.

In 76 games for the Orioles in 1985, Wiggins showed flashes of his talent, but never lived up to his past potential as he batted .285 with 30 stolen bases and 43 runs scored. His production slipped further in 1986 when he batted .251 with 21 stolen bases and 30 runs scored.

By 1987, the Orioles' patience with Wiggins grew thin and he split his time between second base and later designated hitter with the promotion of Billy Ripken. Wiggins received an indefinite suspension from Major League Baseball on September 1, 1987, for what was initially reported as a behavior issue, but is believed to be for a positive

---

2   Tim Raines had 90 for the Expos.

drug test. He was released soon after, despite the team having to pay most of his salary for the 1988 season.

Wiggins would never return to the major leagues, and died on January 6, 1991, due to complications from AIDS. The one-time professional athlete would weigh less than 75 pounds at the time of his death. He reportedly contracted AIDS via intravenous drug use. Wiggins, the father of retired WNBA player Candice Wiggins, became the first major league baseball player known to have died from AIDS.

Author Jeff Seidel echoed the sentiments many felt about the Orioles at this point. The team that appeared to do no wrong for nearly twenty years now appeared to do almost nothing right. Just about every move they made in attempt to compete for the division back-fired and only pushed the franchise further behind the competition.

"The Orioles had lost their way after the 1983 season," Seidel said. "Their farm system dried up and the young talent was just not there like it had been from 1966 to 1983, when they were the best team in baseball who went to six World Series and won three of them."

The poor personnel decisions became even more apparent during the 1986 season, as the team finished in last place in the AL East with a record of 73–89, which was 22 1/2 games behind the first-place Boston Red Sox.

Surprisingly, the Orioles were in contention for much of the season and were in second place in the division with a record of 59–47 on August 5, just 2 1/2 games out of first place. But the team would tumble after that, losing 42 of their final 56 games. The season would represent the final campaign for Weaver, who would retire from the Orioles for a second time. The 1986 season would also represent the only losing season for the Orioles in seventeen years with Weaver at the helm, who was affectionately known as "The Earl of Baltimore."

Sportscaster Keith Mills said the Orioles of the mid-to-late 1980s were a shell of their former selves. Mills, who spent twenty years at WMAR-TV and more than a decade working for WBAL-TV and WBAL-AM radio, said team ownership was looking for a quick fix, which led to hasty decisions that put the franchise in a deeper hole. Instead, the Orioles should have concentrated on developing a long-term rebuilding plan.

"There wasn't the same investment in the farm budget and there was a slow erosion in the talent coming out of the minors," Mills said. "The team lost scouts and player development people, and those that followed them didn't bring in the right players.

"The Orioles then tried to get into the free agent market aggressively for the first time ever and missed really badly on a lot of players," Mills continued. "The players they brought in were either injured, past their prime, underperformed, or were just not what the team needed in order to succeed. By the 1987 and 1988 seasons most of the players on the roster were not ones developed by the team. That's not what the Oriole Way was all about.

"When I first started covering the team in 1980, it was like a family in the clubhouse. Things changed considerably by 1985, and the bottom dropped out of the franchise by 1988. Many of these players came in with a whole different mindset than previous generations. Orioles fans were not used to this type of losing. Free agency just did not work out well for the team and there was no true sense of what they should be doing."

Frustrated by the losing and the lack of home-grown talent to fill the voids, then-Orioles owner Edward Bennett Williams continued to push general manager Hank Peters to reach on free agents. While the free agents may have been names with established track records, they were mostly on the downside of their careers. Ripken Jr. said the Orioles should have concentrated on rebuilding, but ownership believed they were just a player or two away each season.

"In 1985, we go out and sign Don Aase, Lee Lacy, and Freddie Lynn, and we had the hitting, but the pitching wasn't quite there at this point," Ripken said. "Overall, at that point, the structure of the whole team and organization began to change.

"Where before we were getting the timely hits, moving runners over, or getting a timely pitching performance, it wasn't happening in 1986," Ripken Jr. continued. "They then bring Earl back [after firing Joe Altobelli] as manager in 1985 and we played well for much of 1986 before having an awful end to the season. Earl then walked away believing that even he could not fix the team at that point."

The team's sense of desperation was evident in 1987 with the signings of second baseman Rick Burleson and third baseman Ray Knight. Burleson, who signed a one-year, $475,000 deal, was a Gold Glove winner and four-time All-Star. However, injuries limited him to just 137 games between 1982 and 1986 for the Angels before joining the Orioles as a thirty-six-year-old free agent. Burleson batted just .209 in 59 games before being released during the All-Star break.

Knight was thirty-four years old when he signed a two-year, $1 million deal with the Orioles. The signing of the two-time All-Star came a season after Knight was named the World Series MVP with the New York Mets. Knight actually fared pretty well during his one season in Baltimore, batting .256 with 14 home runs and 65 RBIs while appearing in 150 games.

The free agent signings did little to change the Orioles' fortune. If anything, it sent the franchise continuing toward its downward spiral. While they actually fared better in the standings—finishing sixth in the AL East in 1987—the team did worse in the win-loss column, finishing with a record of 67–95 in Cal Ripken Sr.'s first season as manager.

"The 1987 season was my first in Baltimore, so I wasn't there for the glory years, but I was aware of where the Orioles once stood," said

Ken Rosenthal, a former *Baltimore Sun* Orioles beat writer, baseball reporter, and columnist who is now a national baseball writer for *The Athletic*. "It was obvious the team was heading in the wrong direction, but no one could have predicted what was coming in 1988."

Baltimore sports historian Mike Gibbons said there were several competing factors in play that led to the decline of the Orioles in the mid-to-late 1980s.

"The biggest thing that occurred between 1983 and 1988 was that the team simply got old and old really fast," Gibbons said. "I've talked with Hank Peters in the past many times and wanted to know how the team slid so far in just five years. The general manager told me he had been opposed to jumping into the free agent market originally but went out and signed Fred Lynn and Lee Lacy among other players during that time. However, the ownership at the time wanted to move in a different direction and make a concerted effort to bring in proven all stars who could help the Orioles win now."

Gibbons said there were severe disagreements between the front office and the ownership about which direction to move the organization heading into the future. Those disagreements likely expedited the team's decline and affected the course of the franchise for years to come.

"Hank Peters said it was by design that the Orioles took focus away from the farm system and put more resources into going after free agents," Gibbons continued. "The move took the Orioles away from what led them to all those World Series appearances and championships and played a role in their demise in 1988."

At the end of the day, there was an internal squabble between Hank Peters and Edward Bennett Williams. And as history has shown, it was ownership who won in the end, as Peters was gone by 1987.

Baltimore attorney and sports agent Ron Shapiro said the combination of him still having many Oriole players as clients and the team being the one he cheered for in his youth made it even more difficult to see the direction the franchise was heading. It was apparent the Orioles needed to alter their course if it was going to be successful in the future.

"As things went downhill after that season, it was difficult to watch and was very disappointing for myself and the players," Shapiro said. "Everything changed in 1975 when free agency entered the game and the ability to keep teams together became more difficult. At the same time, it provided players opportunities to move that they did not have before and freedoms that they still have to this day."

A fourth straight disappointing season led Williams to make even more changes which helped set the stage for the train wreck of a season that was 1988 for the Orioles. Mills said the moves made by ownership and the front office during this period had a negative effect on the Orioles for arguably decades to follow.

"Edward Bennett Williams and Hank Peters just had a difference of opinion on what approach to take toward the end," Mills said. "Hank Peters was the perfect person to take over for Frank Cashen to continue the Oriole Way, but free agency changed everything. The effects of some of the mistakes made leading up to the 1988 season were felt for decades, especially as it relates to the farm system. We have seen signs that that has changed in recent years with the emergence of players like Manny Machado, Trey Mancini, and Zach Britton among others, but it took time, a really long time."[3]

Longtime Baltimore newspaper columnist Michael Olesker agreed with that assessment by Mills. Olesker, a Baltimore native who worked for the *Baltimore Sun*, *Baltimore News-American*, *Baltimore Examiner*, and WJZ-TV, said the Orioles needed much more than a quick fix by the late 1980s.

"As the Orioles were struggling, team owner Edward Bennett

---

3   Since this interview, Machado and Britton are no longer with the club.

Williams was dying [of cancer]. He was looking for a quick fix to turn things around, and there are just no quick fixes in baseball. The Orioles reached on over-the-hill and oft injured free agents like Don Aase, Lee Lacy, and Fred Lynn, and it just did not work out. They had completely gotten away from the Oriole Way and it showed on the field.

"The Orioles, who were so used to building teams through the farm system, just could not adjust to the period of free agency," Olesker continued. "Look at 1976. That season, they traded away home-grown Don Baylor for Reggie Jackson, who was a year away from free agency and did not want to play in Baltimore. He actually sat out the start of the season and missed several weeks before finally signing with the team, only to leave for the New York Yankees a year later."

Chapter Two

SETTING THE STAGE FOR ROCK BOTTOM

More major changes began on October 5, 1987, when Orioles team owner Edward Bennett Williams announced during an 11 a.m. news conference that he had fired general manager Hank Peters and farm system director Tom "T-Bone" Giordano. At the same time, Williams announced that Cal Ripken Sr. would return for a second season as the team's skipper.

The firing ended a 12-year run by Peters with the Orioles. During his tenure, the Orioles averaged 89 wins a year and before 1984 only finished lower than second place once.[1]

Williams had reportedly grown impatient with Peters's decision-making process and believed the farm system had been poorly managed for several years. Despite the success over more than a decade

---

[1]   Though the Orioles completed the 1978 season with a 90–71 record, they finished in 4th place behind the Milwaukee Brewers (93–69), Boston Red Sox (99–64), and the New York Yankees (100–63).

13

at the helm, Peters seemed resigned to the fact that it was time for a change in Baltimore.

"I'm relieved to be relieved," Peters famously told reporters at the time of his firing.

A little more than a month later, the team announced that veteran baseball executive Roland Hemond would replace Peters as general manager. A baseball lifer, Hemond had spent the previous two years as a special assistant to MLB commissioner Peter Ueberroth. However, he was most well-known for his 15-year tenure as general manager of the Chicago White Sox from 1970 to 1985, which included winning the AL West Division title in 1983.

In addition to Hemond, the new faces in the front office heading into the 1988 season included farm director Doug Melvin, vice president Larry Lucchino, and Hall of Famer Frank Robinson, who was brought into the organization as an assistant general manager. Hemond came to Baltimore with a reputation for being willing to make deals. So, with a team coming off its worst season in thirty-two years, the Orioles were a franchise in need of such a shake-up.

Roy Firestone said the club had gotten so far away from what made them successful that it would be hard for even the most veteran and successful front office personnel to turn the franchise around in the short term. They were a team without an identity. Furthermore, it seemed like every chance they took on a risky player failed to deliver and may have even set the franchise back even further in certain instances.

"The free agent gambles did not pay off and it really set the Orioles back after 1983," Firestone said. "This paved the way for the 1988 season, which was just as horrendous a season as a team could possibly have. When you make bad choices in free agency and drafting, lose quality personnel people, and get old in other areas on the field, it is a recipe for disaster. That's what happened in 1988.

Generally speaking, other teams caught up with the Orioles when it came to personnel and player development and then surpassed them."

Some of Hemond's early dealings would pay dividends, while others did little to help the team either in the short- or long-term. On November 6, 1987, Hemond traded infielders Rico Rossy and Terry Crowley Jr. to the Pittsburgh Pirates for right fielder Joe Orsulak. Orsulak would be in the starting lineup on Opening Day in 1988 and would remain an integral member of the Orioles through the 1992 season. Known for his blue-collar work ethic, Orsulak is still considered one of the most popular players in team history.

At that point in his career, Orsulak said, he was just happy to know he would likely have a spot on a major-league roster on Opening Day. He knew that his new club had struggled in recent years and he did not expect to be competing for a postseason spot, but also had no idea what was on the horizon in 1988.

"I'm not sure exactly how we got to that point in 1988," Orsulak said. "For one, it did not seem like the minor league system was producing players like it used to. When you don't have that, it can have a negative effect on a club for years. That combined with players getting injured, free agents not working out, and others who you expect production from not giving it to you, can spell disaster for a season."

Around three months later, on February 27, 1988, third baseman Ray Knight was dealt to the Detroit Tigers for veteran pitcher Mark Thurmond. Thurmond would spend two seasons with the Orioles, dividing his time between the bullpen and starting rotation. In 1988, Thurmond posted a 1–8 record with a 4.58 ERA in 43 games (including six starts). The following season he went 2–4 with a 3.90 ERA in 49 games, while being used primarily as a relief pitcher. Thurmond was out of baseball after the 1991 season before joining his family's insurance business in Texas.

The biggest trade pulled off by Hemond heading into the 1988 season came on March 21, when he sent outfielder Mike Young and a player to be named later[2] to the Philadelphia Phillies for infielder Rick Schu and outfielders Keith Hughes and Jeff Stone.

Schu, who was once viewed as a possible replacement for Phillies Hall of Famer Mike Schmidt at third base, batted .256 with four home runs and 20 RBIs in 89 games for Baltimore in 1988. He managed to stay in professional baseball until 1997, including stops with the Detroit Tigers, California Angels, Philadelphia Phillies, Montreal Expos, and in Japan from 1993–1994, playing with the Nippon Ham Fighters. He later became a hitting coach for the Arizona Diamondbacks and Washington Nationals before being hired as an assistant hitting coach for the San Francisco Giants entering the 2018 season.

Stone was once considered the prized prospect of the Phillies organization. The initial assessment of the speedster had some calling him a left-handed Ricky Henderson. In 1984, Stone stole 27 bases in just 51 games. While he got his batting average up to .277 with 19 stolen bases in 82 games for the 1986 season, the Phillies lost patience with Stone by 1988, leading to his trade to the Orioles.

To call Stone's lone season with Baltimore a disaster would be a huge understatement. Just twenty-seven years old at the time, Stone batted a paltry .164 with four stolen bases in just 26 games. He actually appeared in 20 of the first 21 games during the losing streak before being shelved with a dislocated middle finger.

Stone began the year in a 1-for-32 slump and played a key role in several of the team's losses during the streak. This included on April 14, 1988, when he misplayed a fly ball off the bat of Frank White that led to the game-winning run in a 4–3 win by the Kansas City Royals.

---

2   The player would be Frank Bellino, who would be sent to Philadelphia three months later, completing the trade.

This miscue came after he failed to get a sacrifice bunt down and was picked off first while going hitless in three at-bats in the game.

Then, on April 19, 1988, Stone was easily thrown out while attempting to go from first to third on an infield grounder in the top of the seventh in a 9–5 loss at the Milwaukee Brewers. After being injured, Stone would not return to the major-league club until mid-September. He would sign with the Texas Rangers in the offseason and was out of professional baseball by 1990.

Also acquired in the offseason was pitcher Jose Bautista. The Dominican Republic native was just twenty-three years old when the Orioles drafted him on December 7, 1987, from the New York Mets in the Rule 5 Draft. Bautista was supposed to develop into one of the anchors of the team's pitching staff of the future. Playing behind a slow, aging defense, Bautista would struggle mightily in his rookie season, posting a 6–15 record with a 4.30 ERA and 76 strikeouts in 171 2/3 innings. The season actually represented Bautista's best year with the club.

It also included the best start of his career when he set the Major League record for fewest pitches in a complete game of eight innings or more. He threw 70 pitches in a 1–0 loss to the Seattle Mariners on September 3, 1988, at the old Kingdome. In that game, Bautista allowed four hits while striking out two. However, Mickey Brantley's one-out RBI double was the difference in that game for the Mariners.

"That 1–0 loss at Seattle was the toughest for me that season," Bautista said. "I pitched the best game of my career and it only took me 70 pitches, but I had nothing to show for it when it was all said and done.

"I spent a lot of time in the clubhouse that night after the game," he continued. "[Former Orioles bullpen coach] Elrod Hendricks was so good to me that night. He stayed with me and reminded me it was just one game and you can't let the bad feelings linger."

Bautista remained with the Orioles through the 1991 season before spending time with the Chicago Cubs, San Francisco Giants, Detroit Tigers, and St. Louis Cardinals, retiring after the 1997 season. After leaving Baltimore, Bautista transitioned into a pretty reliable relief pitcher with his best season coming with the Cubs in 1993 (posting a 10–3 record with a 2.82 ERA in 111 2/3 innings). In 2018, Bautista served as the pitching coach for the Kannapolis Intimidators, the Single-A affiliate of the Chicago White Sox.

Two days after the Orioles acquired Bautista, the team would trade pitcher Ken Dixon to the Mariners for veteran pitcher Mike Morgan. Morgan, who was twenty-eight at the time, showed the ability to be an innings eater by throwing a combined 423 1/3 innings for the Mariners between 1986 and 1987—despite the fact that he lost 17 games in each of those seasons (leading the league in that category for the '86 season).

Morgan had one of the worst seasons of his 25-year career with the Orioles in 1988 after back-to-back 17-loss seasons when he posted a 1–6 record with a 5.43 ERA in just 71 1/3 innings. Morgan would be traded to the Dodgers in the offseason and would go on to be one of the most well-traveled players in major-league history. Nicknamed "The Nomad," Morgan would pitch for a dozen different clubs before retiring after the 2002 season.

Additional players who played a significant role on the Opening Day roster would be acquired in 1987 at the expense of players who were vital contributors to the 1983 World Series team. This included catcher Terry Kennedy and pitcher Mark Williamson (who were acquired on October 30, 1986, from the San Diego Padres in exchange for starting pitcher Storm Davis).

Kennedy, who was thirty-one at the time of the trade, batted .250 with 18 home runs and 62 RBIs in 1987. However, his production dropped off in 1988 when he batted .226 with three home runs in just 85 games. Kennedy, who was signed to replace 1983 World Series MVP Rick Dempsey, was traded on January 24, 1989, to the San Francisco Giants for catcher Bob Melvin.

Williamson, who was twenty-seven, went on to spend his entire eight-year major-league career with the Orioles. Mainly used out of the bullpen, the right-hander compiled a career record of 46–35 with a 3.86 ERA, 397 strikeouts, and 21 saves. Among the highlights of his career was July 13, 1991, when he combined with pitchers Bob Milacki, Mike Flanagan, and Gregg Olson for a no-hitter against the Oakland Athletics. It was the last time the Orioles posted a no-hitter heading into the 2019 season.

Flanagan was dealt less than a year after Davis, being sent to the Toronto Blue Jays on August 31, 1987, for pitcher Oswaldo Peraza and a player to be named later. (Pitcher Jose Mesa was sent by Toronto to complete the deal on September 4, 1987.) Peraza was a twenty-five-year-old hard-throwing righty from Venezuela, posting a 5–7 record with a 5.55 ERA in 86 innings for the Orioles in 1988. Peraza missed the entire 1989 season due to injuries, never made it out of the minor leagues again, and retired after the 1992 season.

Mesa would spend five largely uneventful seasons with the Orioles, where he never gained traction as a starting pitcher. Baltimore traded him to the Cleveland Indians in 1992, where he eventually blossomed into one of the better closers in baseball. A two-time All-Star, Mesa led the American League with 46 saves with the Indians in 1995. He went on to save 321 games while also playing for the Giants, Mariners, Pirates, Rockies, Tigers, and Phillies before retiring in 2007. Coincidentally, Mesa's son, twenty-four-year-old Jose Mesa Jr., entered 2018 trying to make the Orioles pitching rotation after the team acquired him as a Rule 5 Draft pick from the Yankees in December 2017.

The Orioles also tried to bolster their bullpen in 1987 when they traded center fielder John Shelby and pitcher Brad Havens on May 22 to the Dodgers for closer Tom Niedenfuer. Niedenfuer's best season came in 1985 when he had 19 saves and 102 strikeouts with a 2.71 ERA. He struggled initially when he arrived in Baltimore, posting a 3–5 record with a 4.99 ERA, but fared better in 1988 when he led the team with 18 saves to go along with a 3.51 ERA. Niedenfuer, who married actress Judy Landers, signed with the Seattle Mariners after the 1988 season and retired two years later.

Offensively, Hemond made one of his shrewdest signings at the start of the 1988 season. That was when he acquired catcher Mickey Tettleton a week after he had been released by the Oakland Athletics. He would play two seasons with the Orioles before being dealt after the 1990 season to the Detroit Tigers for pitcher Jeff Robinson. A two-time All Star, Tettleton would finish his career with 245 home runs and 732 RBIs, while also playing for the Rangers before retiring after the 1997 season.

By the time Hemond was done dealing, the Orioles Opening Day roster in 1988 would include just eleven players who were on the team's Opening Day roster the previous season.

"Roland Hemond knew changes needed to be made and he took a lot of chances to re-tool the Orioles roster heading into the 1988 season," Ken Rosenthal said.

Jeff Seidel said the result of years of mismanagement—from player development to the front office—was about to rear its head in an ugly way.

"All of those missteps came to a head in 1988," said Seidel, whose reporting on the Orioles led to him co-authoring *Skipper Supreme*. "Most people felt they would not be a good team in 1988, but I don't think given some of the players they still had—like Cal Ripken Jr. and Eddie Murray—people realized just how bad they were going to be in 1988."

Mike Gibbons said there was hope from some people in the organization that the latest shakeup within the organization would give the team the spark it needed to compete again in the AL East.

"The Orioles were still OK in 1984 and 1985, but you could see signs of trouble on the horizon," Gibbons said. "By 1986 and 1987 the team was simply meddling along, and it was obvious they were heading backward. Still, there were some talented players on the roster and it was not apparent about just how bad the Orioles were going to be entering the 1988 season."

Chapter Three

SIGNS OF TROUBLE

As the Orioles reported for Spring Training in 1988, most of those familiar with the team knew they were likely going to struggle throughout the season.

Along with coming off a sixth-place finish, the Orioles were next to last in the AL in runs scored (729) despite being third in home runs (211). Compounding the lack of offense was a pitching staff that ranked next to last in ERA at 5.01. In addition, the roster was extremely slow, finishing last in stolen bases in the AL with 69 in 1987. The league average that season was 124.

Even with several experienced hurlers on the roster, the pitching staff remained a source of concern heading into spring training. Scott McGregor appeared all but done in 1988 after posting a 2–7 record with a 6.64 ERA the previous season. However, he managed to make the Opening Day roster thanks to a strong performance during Spring Training.

At the same time, young pitchers who were expected to contribute failed to impress the coaching staff. This included hurlers like John

Habyan, Eric Bell, and Jeff Ballard, who each started the 1988 season in the minors. Ballard said the Orioles had also placed their hope—and much of their future—on some of the young power pitchers they had acquired in recent years.

"The team really had a change in philosophy heading into the 1988 season as they were looking for harder-throwing pitchers, which they thought they had in guys like Jose Bautista and Oswaldo Peraza," Ballard said. "They were trying to get away from just having control pitchers in the rotation. I had no chance to make the team out of Spring Training as I didn't deserve to be up there."

Habyan was the Orioles' third-round pick in the 1982 MLB Amateur Draft out of St. John the Baptist High School in West Islip, New York. He originally debuted for the Orioles in 1985, but split time between the minors and majors through 1988. His most productive year with the Orioles came in 1987, when he posted a record of 6–7 with a 4.80 ERA in 27 games, which included 13 starts.

Habyan said by the time 1988 came around, it was apparent the Orioles were a team in steep decline, one he was not sure was going to reverse course anytime soon.

"We had success in the minor leagues every step of the way and felt pretty good about ourselves coming up through the system," said Habyan. "I think by the time I got close to the majors, the team was getting older and was trying to get back to where they once were.

"I was a young pitcher who was told to throw strikes and get outs with contact. That is a hard thing to accomplish when for the most part the team was old and slow," Habyan continued, who entered 2019 as the pitching coach at Hofstra University in New York. "A team needs good defense when the pitching may have problems or good pitching when the defense may have problems. Our problem was our pitching and defense had problems. You are not going to win when both the pitching and defense are bad."

Former Orioles pitcher Jose Bautista shared a similar sentiment. Bautista said while the team had a lot of name recognition on paper, the roster was poorly constructed and included many players who were on the team more for past accomplishments than current production and contributions.

"There were a lot of names on that team, but we also had a lot of players whose best days were far behind them," Bautista said. "There were a lot of old, slow players on the roster and it cost us some games during the early part of the season. That was a really bad experience for me over the course of that season, especially being a rookie."

A combination of injuries to key players, impatience by the owner, rushing young players through the system, and hoping older players recaptured past glory all came together to give the Orioles a confluence of reasons why the 1988 season was destined to be a disaster. The signs were there as Spring Training progressed and the Orioles lost nineteen games during Grapefruit League play.

"It was obvious in Spring Training that the Orioles were far from being contenders," Ken Rosenthal said. "But there was still some talent on the roster, especially with Cal and Eddie in the middle of the lineup. It wasn't like the Orioles didn't have players, but this was far from the team that won the World Series just five years earlier."

Even with those concerns, some of the veterans on the roster believed there was enough talent with championship experience to surprise the critics heading into the season. Outfielder Fred Lynn was one of those players. He said he left Spring Training with the same sense of optimism he felt in every other season of his long, successful career. However, with hindsight being 20/20, Lynn admits he could not have been more wrong in his assessment.

"Spring Training is typically a time for optimism, and I had no reason to feel differently in 1988," Lynn said. "I looked around and felt we had some good players. There were some concerns about the pitching, but there was still reason for optimism. I did not think we were a last-place team and felt if enough things broke our way we could compete for the playoffs.

"That is the way you're supposed to feel going into a baseball season from Spring Training. The roster wasn't a group of rookies and up-and-comers," Lynn continued. "We had some solid veterans on that team. There was Cal Ripken Jr. and Eddie Murray, of course. Plus, we had myself and Billy Ripken, along with some veteran pitchers like Mike Boddicker, Scottie McGregor, and Mike Morgan who each knew how to win at the big-league level."

Scott Garceau, a sportscaster and play-by-play voice in Baltimore, admits he also entered the 1988 season looking through the lenses of the proverbial orange and black tinted glasses. Garceau, who was part of the team's television broadcast team for several seasons, including in 1988, said he thought given the veterans on the pitching staff, the Orioles had the chance to at least hover around .500.

"Coming out of spring training that year, I thought the pitching may be better than most had thought and believed they had a chance to be somewhat competitive," said Garceau. "Boy was I wrong, and I was reminded of that by others very early in the season."

Fellow sportscaster Keith Mills admittedly is an eternal optimist when it comes to the hometown teams. However, in this case, Mills said he went into the 1988 season with more concerns than he may have had in previous years.

"Toward the end of Spring Training in 1988, I ran into [Orioles manager] Cal [Ripken] Sr. in Florida," Mills said. "Typically, managers are full of optimism at that time of the year, but he was just depressed. He said to us that did not know how they were going to fare because they just didn't have the pitching. He had no idea they would be that bad."

Chapter Four

OPENING DAY STRUGGLES

Having the start of the baseball season during the spring is simply poetic. The spring symbolizes a new beginning as temperatures begin to warm, flowers begin to bloom, and leaves reappear on trees. Opening Day is also the most optimistic time for baseball fans. It is a time when every team has the same record, that hope springs eternal and the belief that anything is possible—even for the teams expected to struggle the most.

Fans of the Baltimore Orioles were no exception to this belief when they hosted then-AL East rival Milwaukee Brewers for Opening Day on April 4, 1988. A franchise-record 52,395 fans packed Memorial Stadium to see their team begin the season anew.

Even though the Orioles had lost a combined 184 games the previous two seasons, the memories of 1983 and the World Series were not too distant in the minds of many fans. Plus, with holdovers such as shortstop Cal Ripken Jr., first baseman Eddie Murray, pitchers Scott McGregor and Mike Boddicker, along with veteran additions like outfielder Fred Lynn and catcher Terry Kennedy, and up-and-comers like second baseman Billy Ripken and right fielder Joe Orsulak on the roster, there was some belief that the Orioles could at least be competitive if everything broke in their favor.

Still, the margin for error was small and the patience of the team's fans and front office was wearing thin with hopes of a turn-around for the once dominant franchise. Getting off to a strong start on Opening Day was vital to lay the foundation for the season. The Orioles appeared to have the right pitcher on the mound for them in Boddicker. The team's ace, Boddicker had won a combined 56 games and averaged more than 200 innings pitched the previous four seasons.

Everything seemed to be going well during the first three innings against the Brewers. The veteran hurler allowed three singles during that time but stayed out of trouble and did not allow a run. At the same time, the Orioles offense was not doing much as their hitters struck out five times off Brewers ace Teddy Higuera.

A sign of things to come came in the top of the fourth when catcher B. J. Surhoff led off the inning with a line drive single to center field. Boddicker then hit first baseman Greg Brock before left fielder Rob Deer hit a double to left field to drive in Surhoff for the first run of the season. Right fielder Glenn Braggs followed Deer by hitting into a double play before third baseman Ernie Riles drove in Deer with a single to right field to give the Brewers a 2–0 lead.

Boddicker allowed two more runs in the top of the fifth and pitched to just two batters in the sixth before being replaced by Oswaldo Peraza. Boddicker exited having allowed four runs on nine hits while striking out two and walking two in 5 1/3 innings pitched.

Neither Peraza nor Dave Schmidt, who replaced Peraza, fared

much better. The pitchers each gave up four runs apiece over the next two innings. Schmidt's day on the mound was particularly rough. He replaced Peraza with one out in the eighth and promptly got designated hitter and future Hall of Famer Paul Molitor to ground out to second.

But it was all downhill from there, as center fielder Robin Yount, another future Hall of Famer, walked, then Surhoff and Brock singled, the latter driving in Yount. Surhoff would score one batter later after Deer doubled to left. Schmidt then threw a wild pitch with Braggs at the plate and Brock scored. Riles capped the day's scoring for the Brewers one batter later when his single to right allowed Deer to score. Schmidt's final line: four runs on four hits with one walk in 1 1/3 innings. His ERA for the game: a jaw-dropping 108.0.

On the flip side, the Orioles' offense had virtually no answer for Higuera, who scattered three hits over seven innings while striking out seven and walking one in a game the Brewers went on to win by a score of 12–0.

The Orioles managed just five hits and only slightly threatened to score in the bottom of the eighth, when Kennedy led off with a single off reliever Mark Clear. Orsulak followed Kennedy with a single to right before outfielder Jeff Stone flied out to right and second baseman Billy Ripken grounded into a double play to end the inning. By comparison, the Brewers finished with sixteen hits. By the end of the day, every Milwaukee starter had at least one hit.

"It was a brutal way to start the season," Ken Rosenthal said. "Everything that could go wrong did go wrong. At the same time, it was just one game so there wasn't a sense of panic yet."

The loss tied the record at the time for the most lopsided Opening Day shutout in American League history. It was also the first time the Orioles had ever been shut out on Opening Day, something through

2017 they had only done one other time, a 7–0 loss to the Brewers to start off the 1995 season.[1]

Orsulak said the Opening Day loss was a tough game to play in, especially with it being a sold-out contest in their home stadium. He added that the loss was a warning that the worst of the season was still to come.

"The loss on Opening Day really set the tone from the outset," Orsulak said. "You hope it is only one game, but to lose like that on Opening Day in front of your hometown fans is a tough pill to swallow—even thirty years later."

As tough as the loss was, most of the players and coaches were not yet ready to hit the panic button. After all, it was just the first of 162 on the schedule, and there would be plenty of chances to right the ship.

Or so they thought.

"The Opening Day in 1988 was the worst one I can remember being in over my career," Lynn said. "Losing 12–0 in front of your home fans is a tough way to start the season. But, once it was over, we just shook it off and reminded ourselves it was just one game in the course of a long season. The problem after that, though, was obviously that it turned out to be more than just one game."

Little did the Orioles realize that their first loss was just a sign of things to come. Things were set to go from bad to worse to historically awful in just the span of a few weeks in April. Veteran sportscaster Roy Firestone said it was obvious from the first game of the season that 1988 was going to be a long year for the Orioles and their fans.

"The Orioles were just horrible from Opening Day with that

_____

1   The current MLB record for the worst shutout loss on Opening Day was set in 2016, when the Los Angeles Dodgers handed the San Diego Padres a 15–0 defeat to kick off the season.

12–0 loss to the Brewers, which was at the time the worst shutout loss ever on Opening Day," Firestone said. "That loss was simply a harbinger of things to come in 1988. That whole season was simply hideous. There is no other way to describe it."

12-0 loss to the Browns, which was at the time the worst shutout loss ever on Opening Day," Firestone said. "That loss was simply a harbinger of things to come in 1988." That whole season was simply hideous. There is no other way to describe it.

Chapter Five

THE FIRING OF CAL SR.

Cal Ripken Sr. waited thirty-six years for the chance to have his dream job: manager of the Baltimore Orioles. In many ways, that dream turned into a nightmare as soon as he took over the reins from Earl Weaver in 1987.

Instead of a roster filled with the likes of Brooks Robinson, Frank Robinson, Boog Powell, and Jim Palmer, Ripken's roster was filled with players who, for the most part, were nowhere near that level. Combined with the arrival of Roland Hemond as general manager, things did not bode well for a baseball lifer such as Ripken.

Born December 17, 1935, in Aberdeen, Maryland, Ripken signed with the Orioles in 1957. A catcher, Ripken made his way up through the minor league system, but injuries would curtail his playing career by 1964 before he would ever reach the majors. He had already begun to make the transition into coaching and began to work his way up the Orioles organizational ladder.

Ripken first became a manager in 1963 when he took over the Fox Cities Foxes of the Class B Illinois-Indiana-Iowa League. He later went on to manage the Aberdeen Pheasants (1963–1964, 1966), the Tri-City Atoms (1965), the Miami Marlins (1967), the Elmira Pioneers (1968), Rochester Red Wings (1969–1970), the Dallas-Fort Worth Spurs (1971), and the Ashville Orioles (1972–1974).

Ripken reached the major leagues in 1976 when the Orioles named him their bullpen coach. He would take over as the team's third-base coach in 1977 when Billy Hunter left to become manager with the Texas Rangers, a role he would remain in through the 1986 season (before Peters named him skipper).

During his tenure as a member of the Orioles coaching staff, Ripken was also with the team when they lost to the Pittsburgh Pirates in seven games of the 1979 World Series and with the team when they won it all in 1983. Ripken had hoped to take over as manager in 1983 after Earl Weaver retired (the first time), but owner Edward Bennett Williams and Peters opted for Joe Altobelli, who had previously managed in the majors from 1977–1979 with the San Francisco Giants, posting a 225–239 record.

To many of the Oriole greats who came up through the minor-league system—from Jim Palmer to Eddie Murray to Boog Powell—it was Cal Ripken Sr. who helped instill the Oriole Way in them. Many of those players credited Ripken with the success in their respective careers.

While wins were difficult to come by during Ripken's tenure as manager, those years did provide him with the highlight of his career. On July 11, 1987, Ripken had the first opportunity to manage two of his three sons—Cal Jr. and Billy—for the first time with the Orioles. Cal Sr. and Cal Jr. had been together with the organization since the younger Ripken arrived in Baltimore in 1981, and Billy Ripken was called up after the All-Star break.

Baltimore attorney and sports agent Ron Shapiro said seeing Cal Ripken Sr. finally get his chance to manage, especially at a time when two of his sons were on the roster, provided a bright spot to an otherwise difficult era in Orioles baseball history.

"I was so happy in 1987 when Cal Sr. finally accomplished his dream of becoming manager of the Orioles," Shapiro said. "It was magnified that much more that he got to manage alongside two of his sons in Cal Jr. and Billy."

Publicly, Ripken Sr. tried to be optimistic and give the fans hope that the 1988 team would at least be competitive. However, the longtime coach and manager knew his team was likely in for a long season even coming out of Spring Training. Many of those in the local media who covered the team knew how concerned Ripken was regarding his team's chances to succeed. Pitching and lack of team speed were two of the greatest concerns Ripken had coming out of Spring Training, according to those who reported on the team regularly.

After the Orioles lost to the Milwaukee Brewers on Opening Day, the team's struggles continued. Two days later, they lost to the Brewers again, this time by a 3–1 margin. A road trip to the Cleveland Indians appeared to be just what the Orioles needed to right the sinking ship. Instead, the four-game series proved to be the demise of Ripken's managerial career.

The Orioles offense struggled mightily, and the pitching was just as bad as it had been against the Brewers. Over the four-game series, the Orioles were outscored 28–6. Baltimore made Cleveland pitchers Scott Bailes and Rich Yett look like the second comings of Cy Young, while making quality pitchers like Greg Swindell and Tom Candiotti look even better. The worst game of the series came on April 9, when the Indians won 12–1 in a game where Cleveland pounded out 20 hits and every starter got at least one.

The final game for Ripken as Orioles manager came on April 11, when Baltimore lost 7–2 for the series sweep. An announced crowd of just 15,816 turned out to watch the Orioles lose their sixth straight game to start the season. At the time, the loss tied the team's worst start in franchise history, which was previously set in 1955, their second year in Baltimore. (They went on to lose 97 games that season.)

Ripken Sr. arrived back in Baltimore after the road trip and started to prepare for a six-game homestand against the Indians and Kansas City Royals. He was actually in uniform and filling out his lineup card, only to be told by Hemond that management had decided to make a change at manager and were going to replace him with Frank Robinson.

"Unfortunately, Cal Sr. felt the brunt of the struggles of the team getting fired so early in the 1988 season," Shapiro said. "Much of the blame placed on Cal Sr. was unjustified and it was painful to watch as Cal Jr. and Billy had to continue on with the team after their father was just fired. But all of those involved in the process understood that it was just part of the business of the sport. However, that does not mean they had to like it, and the Ripken sons did not like it. It was their father after all that just lost his job, one that he wanted for so long."

According to media reports, Williams was growing impatient with the sloppy play of the team, which included several base-running errors and an anemic offense that had been outscored 43–7 over six games. The Orioles were also the last team in the majors to hit a home run, finally doing so when third baseman Rick Schu connected on a two-run shot in the fifth against the Indians on April 11.

"It was unfortunate that Cal Sr. finally got the chance to manage the Orioles after being passed over for the job in 1983, only to be fired earlier in the season than any manager ever in baseball history," Ken Rosenthal said. "No manager was going to be able to fix that team, which was obvious when Frank Robinson took over and lost another 15 in a row."

Scott Garceau said while there were rumblings at the time that ownership was considering a managerial move if the Orioles did not show signs of life, he did not believe the firing would occur so early in the season.

"The team had just been swept by the Indians in Cleveland and I did not think it would be a good night for me to go down to the clubhouse," Garceau said. "They were 0–6 at that point of the season, and I went to the team bus and Frank Robinson sat down next to me. I remember talking with him about how much trouble the team was already in this early in the season. They were getting outplayed, were not competitive, and the games were ugly.

"We then fly home and I get a call the next morning at the station to be at the stadium for a press conference because the Orioles had an announcement to make," Garceau continued. "That's when they fired Cal Sr. and hired Frank Robinson, who I had just been sitting with the night before. Unfortunately, it did not get any better for Frank."

The move shocked many players and others associated with the club, who felt it was unfair to make Ripken Sr. be the fall guy so early in the season. Some said it was not the treatment Ripken, who had been so loyal and hard-working for the organization for so long, deserved. Right fielder Joe Orsulak was among that group of players.

"Cal Sr. did not really deserve to get fired at that point in the season after just six games played," Orsulak said. "It was an unnecessary distraction for a team that did not need any distractions. Cal Sr. was a good baseball man that the team's players respected a great deal.

"Say what you will about Frank Robinson as a manager, but remember he still lost fifteen in a row after taking over," Orsulak continued. "It was not the manager out there making throwing errors, dropping fly balls, or striking out with runners in scoring position. That was us, the players. There is no manager who is going to look good when players are making mistakes like that."

Robinson rejoined the Orioles in 1985 as a coach before making the transition to the front office after the 1987 season. He did not return to Baltimore initially with plans of taking over in the clubhouse. Other than being associated with the Orioles, Robinson was a stark contrast from Ripken Sr.

Robinson compiled 2,943 hits and 586 home runs, while winning Most Valuable Player Awards in both leagues over a 21-year career. The first African American manager in MLB history, Robinson had limited success in managerial stints with the Indians (1975–1977) and the San Francisco Giants (1981–1984) before returning to Baltimore. Robinson would later go on to manage the Montreal Expos and Washington Nationals.

Members of the Orioles' roster had plenty of respect for Robinson, but had wished his hiring did not come due to Ripken Sr.'s firing. To most on the team, the roster as constructed was fatally flawed from the start and no manager would have been able to win with that group of players. Ripken Sr. finished his managerial career with the Orioles with a record of 68–101.

"I don't remember a whole lot about that Spring Training other than we had a great deal of respect for Cal Sr. and were happy to see an organizational guy get a chance to manage on the big-league level," relief pitcher John Habyan said. "We were also upset that he lost his job so early in that season."

Jose Bautista was equally disappointed that Ripken Sr. did not get more of an opportunity to manage the club after waiting so long for his opportunity.

"Cal Sr. getting fired was a surprise so early in the season," Bautista said. "I know the general manager has the right to hire and fire whatever coach or manager they want, but it wasn't the manager's fault. He didn't have a lot of good players to work with."

The news of Ripken's firing was especially tough for Cal Jr. and Billy to deal with. The brothers credit their father with instilling in them the work ethic necessary to reach the highest levels of their chosen profession and believed their father, who literally worked his way up from the bottom of the organization, deserved better after giving more than three decades of his life to the team. Billy actually changed his jersey number from three to seven that season as a sign of respect for his father.

Ripken Jr. said he received no advance warning of the decision and was obviously very upset about how the team handled the situation. Still, Ripken Jr. said he knew he still had a job to do, but admits he believes the firing had a negative effect on the team, at least in the short term.

"We were all excited when dad finally got his shot to manage the Orioles in 1987," Ripken Jr. said. "By all accounts, that should have been the start of a rebuilding phase, but the team did not take that approach. We then lost the first six games in 1988 and dad gets fired just like that. We could have gotten a win or two early on if we had gotten a clutch hit here or there, but firing dad after just six games pulled the rug out from under us and exacerbated the situation. We then of course went on to lose another fifteen games in a row before finally winning a game.

"I heard about dad's firing from the team on the radio as I headed to the stadium that day," Ripken Jr. continued. "All of us were shocked that he would get fired so early in the season. I was also very angry. Dad was a very loyal company man. We did not complain when he did not get the manager's job after Earl Weaver retired the first time in 1982. Then dad finally gets a chance to manage, and he gets a team that just was not very good. It was not like we didn't have some players, but it was just not a team where he was put in a position to succeed. That is exactly what happened to him."

With Ripken Sr.'s firing, Robinson became the Orioles' ninth skipper in team history; but was also the team's fourth manager in as many seasons. The Orioles had offered Ripken a position within the organization, which he initially declined. He would later return to the team as third base coach in 1989 and would remain in that role until being let go after the 1992 season. The Orioles would again try to offer Ripken Sr. another role in the organization, but he declined this time and would never coach again in the majors.[1]

Baltimore sports historian Mike Gibbons said while he had nothing against Frank Robinson, the sudden firing of Ripken Sr. did little to help the club. If anything, it may have made a bad situation even worse.

"The abrupt firing of Cal Ripken Sr. was not handled well by the Orioles at that time," Gibbons said. "He was a popular and beloved figure both in the clubhouse and in the community. He was a trusted and hard-working baseball man who was very loyal to the Orioles for many, many years. Having two of his sons on the team at that point in time did not help matters much, either."

Sportscaster Keith Mills said Ripken Sr. was a dedicated coach and manager who deserves as much credit as anybody for much of the Orioles' success through the 1970s and into the early 1980s. Mills believes it was a shame that Ripken Sr. did not receive a better opportunity to manage the Orioles.

"Cal Sr. did not deserve what happened to him at all," Mills said. "This man embodied the Oriole Way. Any player who came up under him—from Eddie Murray to Jim Palmer to Mike Flanagan to Al Bumbry—would credit him with their success and teaching them the

---

1   The Orioles inducted Ripken Sr. into their team Hall of Fame in 1996, along with former owner Jerry Hoffberger and coach Billy Hunter. Ripken died of lung cancer on March 25, 1999. He left behind his wife, Vi, and four children, Cal, Billy, Fred, and Ellen. He was just sixty-three years old.

right way to play the game. By the time he got a chance to manage, the Oriole Way as we all knew it for so long was gone."

As for Frank Robinson, the Orioles hoped the change in managers would give the team the spark they needed to get into the win column. However, it would be several more weeks—and plenty more heartbreaking losses—before that would come close to happening.

Chapter Six

STRUGGLES CONTINUE, LOSSES PILE UP

What made the Orioles' growing losing streak even more difficult to grasp for those within the organization was not just that they kept losing, but *how* they were losing. Inside the clubhouse, they were also trying to answer *why* they were losing. While they had plenty of deficiencies in every aspect of the game, those shortcomings rarely revealed themselves at the same time.

On any given night, the Orioles might have gotten a quality performance from a starting pitcher, only to have the offense fail on them (take Mike Morgan's complete-game loss to the Brewers on April 6). The next night, the offense might have come alive with timely hits in key situations while the starting pitching or the bullpen would fall apart when they needed to get out of an inning (take the Brewers scoring four times in the fifth inning of a game they trailed 5–3 on April 20). Other times, the pitching and hitting would be there only for a poor defensive play or a base-running miscue to be the difference between a win and a loss (take the team's three-error performance in a 4-3 home loss to the Royals on April 14).

To break it down even further, of the Orioles' 21 straight losses, thirteen defeats were by three runs or less, nine were by two runs or less, and four were one-run defeats. Of those one-run defeats, three took place in a row, from April 14 to 16. In other words, much like the Orioles had all season, the team found a way to snatch defeat from the jaws of victory.

"We were just waiting to see how the team was going to lose each night," Ken Rosenthal said. "I've never seen anything like it before or since in my career. As the losses piled up, it was apparent something historic was taking place."

Orioles Hall of Fame third baseman Brooks Robinson, who was a member of the team's television broadcast team on WMAR-TV, said in all his decades in and around baseball he cannot recall a team that found more ways to lose than the Orioles did in the opening weeks of the 1988 season.

"It was hard to watch a team that had been so good for so long struggle like that to start the season," Robinson said. "I just could not believe what I was watching that year with the Orioles. It did not seem possible that a team could lose 21 straight games in a row. You would think there would be one game where they would get a big hit, a ball would bounce their way, or the pitcher would will the team to a win. It just did not happen, and people began to wonder if they would ever win a game."

Robinson said each night during the losing streak he was just dismayed at how many different ways the team found to lose a game.

"It seemed like when the team hit well, the pitching suffered and when the pitching did well, they could not hit the ball," Robinson said. "It was not like there were a lot of blowouts per se; they just managed to find a different way to lose each night. I had never seen a team so unlucky."

The three straight one-run defeats offered a microcosm into just how frustrating the season would become. The first of those three straight one-run losses—the Orioles' ninth straight defeat—came against the Kansas City Royals. In one of the more dramatic games of the streak, the Royals jumped out to a 3–0 lead after three innings against pitcher Mike Boddicker.

The Orioles then responded in the bottom of the fifth when Fred Lynn connected on a one-out home run off Royals ace Brett Saberhagen, a two-time Cy Young Award winner. Baltimore then tied the game at 3–3 in the bottom of the sixth by scoring twice, which included a two-out RBI double by Billy Ripken. Ripken would score one batter later when Cal Ripken Jr. reached first base on an error.

At the same time, Boddicker, despite being called for two balks that led to runs, was pitching a fantastic game. The team's longtime ace retired eighteen-straight batters between the third and ninth innings and would pitch a complete game as he scattered five hits and allowed one earned run with no walks and 10 strikeouts. Yet he still took the loss.

The Orioles' and Boddicker's downfall came with two outs in the top of the ninth when he opened the inning by getting the Royals' top two hitters—first baseman and future Hall of Famer George Brett and right fielder Danny Tartabull—to strike out. Designated hitter Jim Eisenreich followed with a ground ball single to center and second baseman Frank White lifted a fly ball to left, which outfielder Jeff Stone misplayed, allowing Eisenreich to score from first base as Kansas City went on to win the game, 4–3.

The next night, the Cleveland Indians arrived in Baltimore for a three-game series. In the opener, the Orioles actually led 2–1 thanks to a strong second inning, as Lynn led off the frame with a line drive single to left off Indians starter Rich Yett, followed by a two-run home run by designated hitter Larry Sheets.

Scott McGregor appeared to turn back the clock on Father Time for at least one night, as he held the Indians to just one run through seven innings. Unfortunately for the Orioles and McGregor, it all fell apart in the top of the eighth.

The Indians' rally started when center fielder Joe Carter hit a one-out home run to deep left field. McGregor would then give up a double to designated hitter Ron Kittle before being lifted for reliever Doug Sisk. Sisk would quickly give up a single to third baseman Brook Jacoby, which allowed Dave Clark—a pinch runner for Kittle—to score the eventual game-winning run in a 3–2 Indians victory.

The final of those three one-run losses may arguably be the most heartbreaking of them all. The Orioles again got an outstanding pitching performance: this time from Mike Morgan, who allowed no runs on two hits while walking two and striking out four as he faced just three batters over the minimum in a gritty 122-pitch performance over nine innings.

The only problem is the Orioles offense failed to come through again, and Indians starter Greg Swindell was even better for Cleveland on that night. He allowed no runs on seven hits, struck out three, and walked one in a 113-pitch performance over ten innings.

In fact, the only run in the game came in the top of the 11th. Right fielder Cory Snyder led off with a walk from reliever Dave Schmidt, later advancing to second on a passed ball. Schmidt would respond by striking out shortstop Jay Bell and catcher Chris Bando before walking second baseman Julio Franco. With two on and two outs, first baseman Willie Upshaw drove in the eventual game-winning run on a line drive single to center that allowed Snyder to score en route to a 1–0 Indians victory.

Despite going scoreless in 17 straight innings (going back to the previous day's loss), the Orioles had a chance to win the game in the bottom of the 11th. Billy Ripken led off the frame with a single in the final batter faced by Swindell. Two batters later, Eddie Murray hit a double to right that just missed being a home run off reliever Doug Jones. However, Cal Ripken's early season struggles would continue as he lined out to the pitcher before catcher Terry Kennedy, who was pinch hitting for Schu, was called out on strikes to end the game and extend the losing streak.

It was also frustrating for longtime former head trainer Richie Bancells, who worked at every level of the organization over a forty-six-year career.

"In 1983, I was with Rochester and felt a part of that Orioles World Series championship team," Bancells said. "By 1988, I had made my way to the major league club and it worked out great for me in that regard. I felt like I had been on the same journey with many of the players. That losing streak was not necessarily because of an inferior roster, even if they lacked in pitching. It was a little bit of everything."

Bancells said the Orioles were not necessarily playing as poorly as their record indicated. Instead, they were often a team where one mistake, miscue, or simple bad break was their undoing more so than any team in history.

"We were not a young team filled with a bunch of rookies or up-and-comers," Bancells said. "We got good play at times but, when we made a mistake, it cost us big. Then next thing you know we're 0–10, then winless in fifteen games and are wondering what just happened to our season. Still each night we got to the ballpark, we felt this would be the night it was going to end."

Each loss only appeared to magnify the situation, as players pressed hard on the mound, at the plate, and in the field. The losing streak was quickly becoming a national story, with each defeat leading to the addition of more and more reporters who sought credentials to cover what turned out to be a historic stretch of ineptitude by a professional sports team. The Orioles were now being covered by as many reporters as would normally be reserved for those playing in a World Series, not one seeking their first win.

Fred Lynn said it was apparent by the ninth loss of the season that things were spiraling out of control and every move the team made to try and counteract the defeats would only exacerbate the situation even further.

"It wasn't like every game was a blowout loss like on Opening Day," Lynn said. "It was like one day we'd lose 2–1 and the next we would lose 12–10. It seemed like whatever we were doing well in a game wasn't good enough to overcome what we did bad.

"Crazy things would happen in each game," Lynn continued. "It was like Little League during that stretch. We were inventing ways to lose games each night. In all honesty, it became frustrating very quickly. Before we knew it, we were 0–8 and then 0–9 and we're wondering what was happening to our season. We had some quality players who had the ability to win games and had even won championships in the past, but something always went wrong. We had what I thought was a solid core, but for whatever reason we simply did not gel as a team."

Relief pitcher John Habyan said the reason for the streak was simple: the team was poorly constructed and, with few exceptions, was not very talented.

"The bottom line was we just did not have the personnel to get out of that long losing streak," Habyan said. "I'm not sure we were truly 0–21 bad. However, not having the talent in place did not help matters much for us.

"I was on the Rochester shuttle for much of that season, going up and down between the minor leagues and the big-league club," Habyan continued. "As a player in that position, you are keeping an eye on the streak, but you also can't forget you have got a job to do while trying to stay in the majors. The whole organization played a part in that record-setting losing streak."

The team even tried to bring back a key player from their 1983 team in hopes of capturing lightning in a bottle again. On April 12, 1988, they signed outfielder Tito Landrum, who had been released eight days earlier by the Los Angeles Dodgers. Landrum had last played for the Orioles in 1983 after being acquired as a player to be named in a trade with the St. Louis Cardinals for outfielder Floyd Rayford.

Landrum only appeared in 26 games for the team in 1983, when he batted .310 with one home run and four RBIs in 26 at-bats. He is probably most well-known as the player who hit the game-winning home run in the final game of the 1983 ALCS against the Chicago White Sox.

Landrum would re-sign with the Cardinals in the offseason and remained a role player for several more seasons. He was also a key member for the team in their run toward the 1985 World Series, which they lost to the Kansas City Royals. The Cardinals released Landrum in 1987.

Landrum said at the time he was upset to see just how far the Orioles had fallen since his last stint with the ballclub. Still, he was confident they could turn things around.

"There's a lot of pride in the Orioles organization and it's sad to see what is happening in the organization right now," Landrum told Scott Garceau on the *Orioles on Deck* pregame show on April 29, 1988. "But I know things are going to turn around. We sat down and had our own meetings and found that within ourselves collectively we can stay together, and if we do that, we will be OK."

Landrum's second stint with the Orioles was even shorter than his first one. He batted just .125 with three hits, a double, and two

RBIs in 24 at-bats. He was released on May 10, 1988, and would go on to play for several minor-league teams and even in the Mexican league before retiring in 1991.

Jeff Ballard said there was a perfect storm in place that helped set into motion the events that would lead to such an infamous losing streak.

"We were just a bad team back in 1988," Ballard said. "There were struggles on the pitching staff and the defense for the most part was slow and old. Other guys like [catcher] Terry Kennedy and [outfielder] Larry Sheets were more known for hitting than defense. That was a bad combination to have for sure."

The media following the club picked up even more on April 20, 1988. On that date, the team dropped its fourteenth-straight game, an 8–6 defeat against the host Milwaukee Brewers at County Stadium. The loss set the major-league record for a losing streak to start a season. Previously, the record had been thirteen games set by both the 1904 Washington Senators and 1920 Detroit Tigers. Frank Robinson said each game he felt his guys had the ability to win, only for something to change the momentum into the opponents' favor.

In that fourteenth-straight loss, the Orioles were locked in a close game against the Brewers heading into the bottom of the fifth. At that point, they had already rallied from down 3–0 to take a 5–3 lead. But again, it just took one bad inning to turn the tide.

Down by two, Brewers center fielder Robin Yount led off the bottom of the fifth with a home run off Boddicker. B. J. Surhoff then grounded out to first before Greg Brock singled to center. Rob Deer then hit a shallow fly ball that Cal Ripken Jr. appeared to have a read on before losing it the sky as it fell in for a single. The Brewers went on to score four times that inning, driving Boddicker from the game. He would lose his fourth-straight decision to start the season and his ninth-straight decision overall dating back to the previous year.

"When the streak got to nine or ten in a row you could tell the pressure was starting to build and the players were wondering what would happen to cause them to lose that night," Brooks Robinson said. "Losing streaks like that just aren't supposed to happen at the start of a season.

"I was surprised the streak got that big," Robinson continued. "They weren't a World Series contender by any stretch of the imagination that year, but there were still some proven winners like Mike Boddicker and Mike Morgan who you would think would be able to stop a losing streak.

"I remember each game I called on TV during that streak I could point to one moment in the game where I knew it would eventually cause them to lose in the end. It could have been a loop single, an error, or a strikeout in a bad spot of the game. You could just tell it was set to unravel again."

Ken Rosenthal shared a similar sentiment. "There were just crazy circumstances each night," Rosenthal said. "For whatever reason, something went wrong every night and with each loss more and more reporters started following the team. To say this season was a mess for the Orioles was an understatement."

As each defeat set a new mark for futility, the Orioles, who had been the winningest franchise in baseball from 1957 to 1987, would gain even more attention from the general public. Comedian Bill Cosby, who at that point was still the beloved star of the NBC hit sitcom *The Cosby Show*, and even then-President Ronald Reagan would reach out to the team to offer them support and best wishes.

"As the losses piled up, the attention on us got greater and greater and not for the reasons you want as a player," Ripken Jr. said. "We really felt like it was us against the world at that point in time. It just seemed like what could go wrong did go wrong. Something would happen in the course of the game, and we would just think *here we go again*. It was the same thing night after night and day after day for 21 straight games."

Among those cheering on the Orioles the most during the losing streak was disc jockey Bob Rivers, who worked as the morning drive-time host for Baltimore radio station 98 Rock. Rivers, who recently retired from radio and currently lives in Seattle, decided after the team's eleventh-straight loss to stay on the air until the team won.

When Rivers initially made the proclamation, he figured he would be on the air for a day or two tops. Instead, the Orioles would end up losing ten more games in a row, meaning Rivers would remain on the air for 258 straight hours, or 10 days and 18 hours.

"It was a little more than I bargained for, but it was worth it," Rivers said in a May 16, 1988, article for *People* magazine.

Rivers received media attention from across the globe, as reporters from New York to England to Belize wanted to interview the radio personality, who only slept when music played. Supporters for Rivers reached out from all over with signs stating "Free Bob Rivers" popping up all over town.

* * *

As the losing streak became one of the national lead stories, players on the Orioles said there was little finger-pointing in the clubhouse, likely because the team was too shell shocked to be angry. Many of the players said they worked to keep the team closely bonded together.

"From a locker room perspective, it was not horrible," Lynn said. "The problem was we just could not get away from the streak. Whether we were home or away, the losing streak was the number one topic of conversation among fans, media, and everyone else. It was what people were talking about at work, school, church, and even the grocery store.

"Typically, the first two weeks of the season are kind of boring from a news perspective. There's not a lot to talk about," Lynn continued. "Normally, if a team ends up thirty games under .500 it is spread out over the course of the season. For example, a team might win three in a row and then lose seven of ten, win four of five and then lose eleven of sixteen and so on. This was much different and brought a lot of early attention to Baltimore, and obviously not in a good way. We just could not win a game."

Joe Orsulak shared Lynn's assessment of the situation. He said the team felt like they all took a punch in the gut and there was no way to catch their breath and reset the situation.

"I am still not sure how any team can lose twenty-one games in a row," Orsulak said. "I thought going into the season we had at least a decent team with some talented players. But we had several good players who were struggling at the same time and we got into a situation where everything that could go wrong—from dropped fly balls, to throwing errors, to running errors—happened and it all steamrolled from there.

"Mistakes happen on every team, even those that win one hundred games and go to a World Series and win a championship," Orsulak continued. "But usually those mistakes do not happen to the degree that it happened on that 1988 Orioles team. It actually got to the point where I thought we would not win a single game all season. We had enough talent on that team that we should not have lost twenty-one games in a row. I am still not sure how we managed to do that."

Although the clubhouse did not become too splintered during the streak, emotions would still boil over. This included an incident after the team's sixteenth-straight loss, a 13–1 trashing at the hands of the Royals. The Orioles were down 9–0 in the first inning in a game where Morgan allowed six-straight singles and got pulled from the mound before ever recording an out.

Morgan would end up being charged with six of the nine runs in the inning. Dave Schmidt was charged with the other three, as the Royals had nine hits in the frame. The effort was so poor that Frank Robinson reamed out his players during a closed-door session in the clubhouse after the game.

"The most embarrassing thing is how we look to our peers," Kennedy said in a *New York Times* article on April 23, 1988. "But I know what they're thinking, because I've been on the other side. They're thinking, 'Boy, am I glad it's not me.'"

Lynn said the pressure that mounted as the losing streak continued to grow was as heavy as anything he had ever experienced in his long, distinguished career. He said it felt like the entire world was watching them while every team they played did not want to be the first to lose.

"The weight became incredible," Lynn said. "I've played in the seventh game of the World Series and that was not even as stressful as this losing streak. It was just a crushing blow so early in the season. As the streak grew, every game became like the seventh game of the World Series for the team we were playing because they did not want to be the team to lose to us."

Orsulak said being on a team that was losing in such a way was as surreal as anything he experienced in his career. He added that the horde of media covering the team compounded the situation even more.

"Being a part of that losing streak was so embarrassing, especially when the group of reporters grew as the streak got longer and longer," Orsulak said. "It was nice to see the support from fans and others, including the president, but it was embarrassing to be supported for that. I appreciate the message from the president, but that is not why I want the president to reach out to me."

Ripken Jr. said because of how the losing streak became such a national, and even international story, many of the players in the clubhouse rallied together. He said the players felt they were on an island unto themselves and in the end only had each other to lean on during such a trying season.

"Believe it or not, we became more supportive of each other during that time because we knew any support would be coming from inside, not outside the clubhouse," Ripken Jr. said. "We really looked to each other during the losing streak to keep our spirits up.

"We had to support each other because of all of the attention we received," Ripken continued. "Again, there was not any one reason why we kept losing games. It was a different reason each night. We would become close as a team and, surprisingly, the losing streak helped us with chemistry."

Jose Bautista agreed for the most part with Ripken's observations. Bautista believes the team was just dumbfounded at how the losing streak reached such infamous levels.

"There was no arguing in the clubhouse," Bautista said. "Nobody stuck around long enough after the games to argue over the losses. Players just got their showers, grabbed their things, and got the [hell] out of there. We did not really talk about it."

Orsulak agreed that everyone accepted blame during the losing streak, but it did little to dull the pain.

"Despite the obvious frustration and embarrassment, I don't remember there being a lot of hostility or finger-pointing in the clubhouse," Orsulak said. "This was probably because everyone shared responsibility in the streak. You could not point fingers at teammates when you also dropped balls, pitched poorly, or had a throwing error. Everyone on the team was responsible."

After being swept in a three-game series in Kansas City, the Orioles and their traveling media circus headed to Minnesota for a three-game series with the Twins. With the losing streak now at eighteen, the Orioles were trying to grab on to anything that may have helped them reverse their fortunes.

Bautista said the losing streak had taken on a life of its own.

"We just wanted to get that first win," Bautista said. "We would lose every way imaginable. It was a really bad experience and one I would not want any other player to face. We just did not click as a team in any which way. The team was not put together well at all.

"There was so much pressure on the team and individual players as the streak got bigger and bigger," Bautista continued. "The national press was following us the whole time. We were doing our best to win, but we just kept coming up short and the losses piled on."

Nothing seemed to be working as the club dropped the first two games of the series in Minnesota by scores of 4–2 and 7–6.

Orioles general manager Roland Hemond was even willing to accept good luck charms. That charm would arrive to the Metrodome in the eighth inning of the series finale, a game the Orioles would go on to lose 4–2 to extend the losing streak to twenty-one games in a row.

Hemond was wearing a gray champagne-soaked suit that he last wore five years earlier when the Chicago White Sox clinched the AL West title. That suit had remained with the White Sox in the years that followed before team owners Jerry Reinsdorf and Eddie Einhorn sent it to Hemond that day.

At that point in the season, Frank Robinson was willing to try anything to help his team halt the losing streak and put this nightmare start to the season behind them. He said compounding his frustration was his belief that the Orioles players were still putting in the proper effort on the field.

"We really just cheer hard and you pull and you root," Robinson told reporters after the Twins loss. "You root more than you normally would as a manager. I know that they are trying. I know they are trying really hard, and that is what's so tough about it. Each loss is just getting to be tougher and tougher."

Richie Bancells shared Robinson's frustration for the team's difficult start.

"The season just snowballed out of control really fast," Bancells said. "First the tough loss on Opening Day, then Cal Ripken Sr. gets fired six games in and is replaced by Frank Robinson. The pitching just was not there and every night it was something different. You could not make this up if you tried."

Scott Garceau said he felt bad for the players on the roster. He added that the attention from the national media made it even more difficult for the players to forget about the losing streak because they were reminded of it from the time they woke up to the time they got to the ballpark to the time they went to bed. Then, they had to go through it all again the next night.

"Nothing went right during that streak and they seemed to invent ways to play themselves out of games each and every night," Garceau said. "There was a loss early in the season, 12–1, against the Cleveland Indians, and Boddicker balked in two runs. It was just horrible for them."

Keith Mills said the streak had gotten so big that the players were not sure how to respond on the field, to the media, or to the fans. It was as unique a time in the city's sports history as he can ever remember.

"The amount of tension in the clubhouse was immeasurable during the streak," Mills said. "The losing kept coming and it is never good when the players enter the clubhouse wondering how they are going to lose.

"The Orioles had so many problems with fundamentals over that season," Mills continued. "From not getting a bunt down to missing a cutoff throw to getting caught in a rundown, it was a brutal season. It was mind-boggling to anyone who had watched the Orioles for years before that.

"No one knew how to deal with such a streak. It was unprecedented and people on the team were just in a state of shock and disbelief."

Mills said as someone who had followed the Orioles his whole life—both as a fan and broadcaster—he cannot recall a season more difficult to digest that in 1988.

"The season was so difficult to watch and cover because the franchise had gotten so far away from what made it successful from the 1960s through the early 1980s," Mills said. "The team was known for its farm system, player development, and stability. All of that suddenly changed once Edward Bennett Williams bought the team."

While the good luck charm from Hemond did not arrive in time for the series against the Twins, it may have offered the team a little positive energy heading into their weekend series against the Chicago White Sox.

Chapter Seven

FINALLY A WIN FOR THE ORIOLES

The 1988 season was basically over before it started as the team destroyed the previous mark for futility to start a season. The only question that remained was when the streak would finally end.

In reality, there was little anyone in leadership could do at this point. The roster had already been overhauled since the end of the 1987 season, while ownership had replaced the general manager and the general manager had replaced the manager. There were only so many moves Robinson could make, as the minor league system was not necessarily filled with can't-miss prospects the team had previously relied upon. There was also a concern from the front office not to sacrifice the team's future with the belief that many of the team's prior top prospects were rushed to the major leagues, which hindered their chances of success.

Still, many veterans who remained from the team's championship team were trying to give the city's fanbase hope that a turnaround was just around the corner.

"It's all you can do at this point [trying to cope]," former Orioles pitcher Scott McGregor told Scott Garceau during the *Orioles on Deck* pregame show on April 29, 1988, prior to the series opener against the White Sox. "It's beyond the fact of reality. To think you can't win a game in twenty-one games is amazing."

McGregor remained as positive during the losing streak as he did when the team advanced to the World Series in 1979, lost the AL East division on the final day of the season in 1982, and captured the franchise's third championship a year after that.

"The guys, I have to say, I have been proud of them," McGregor told Garceau. "I think we have handled it well. Every game they come out and they have been fired up. We're playing hard. In Minnesota we played hard, but we just can't seem to come up with the big hit, we all know that. The games we've pitched well, we've been in them.

"We've got a lid on that [win] column and we just have to break it loose," McGregor said. "I still have a lot of confidence in the talent we have here. Right now, because of the way we have been playing, we're just a little under their potential. As soon as we get that confidence going again everyone is going to rise back up. I am still looking for a good season."

At the same time, McGregor said prior to the game against the White Sox that it was a difficult time to be an Orioles player and fan. He added that the international media attention was not something anyone on the team relished.

"You're certainly embarrassed about [the losing streak]," McGregor continued. "You just have to keep playing and keep your confidence up. We have definitely become renowned all throughout the country, not that you want it to be that way. You just have to spin off of it and use that and just show what we are made from. We've had some great times and I have had a great career with the Orioles and sometimes you have to go through times like this. But we still have a long way to go."

McGregor also told Garceau that the pressure to end the losing streak was no different than being on the mound with a championship on the line.

"You have to shut all of that stuff out. When you're in the World Series or any kind of situation like that, you still have to take the field and you have to do all of the little things. I've been happy with the fact that that is how we've been playing.

"We haven't been getting blasted out of games and we've had our innings and times that we have been pretty ugly. But we just have to concentrate on doing the right things. We need pitchers to make the right pitches and hitters bunting guys over and doing the basics. I think if we keep our minds on that we're going to play good baseball and [the losing streak] has to break."

Was there anything that could help the Orioles finally win a game? Calls from the president and celebrities had not worked. Neither had prayers or publicity stunts from disc jockeys. At this point, it was up to the players to just find a way to get a win and put this miserable experience behind them.

Pitcher Dave Schmidt said the players were just numb to the losing at that point and were willing to try anything to reverse their fortunes and get back to just playing baseball.

"There would be a passed ball one night, a balk the next, an error in the field or running after that, or we just didn't play well," said Schmidt, who has coached for the Orioles for about two decades and entered the 2018 season as the team's Florida and Latin American pitching coordinator.

Schmidt said manager Frank Robinson called him and fellow pitcher Mark Williamson into his office after the team's loss against the Twins, their twenty-first in a row. Schmidt said Robinson was brief and to the point for the series opener against Chicago.

"After we lost our twenty-first game in a row, Frank Robinson pulls myself and Mark Williamson into his office and tells us, 'Mark you are starting tomorrow and are going to go six innings. Dave, you are going to pitch the final three innings and we are going to end this tomorrow," Schmidt said. "We leave the room and wonder how we are going to do that because Mark wasn't even a starter. But that's exactly how it played out."

That plan might have sounded over-simplified, but the team appeared ready to put the losing streak to rest. At the same time, the Chicago White Sox appeared to be the right team at the right time for them to play. Much like the Orioles, the White Sox were in the playoffs in 1983.[1]

But just like the Orioles, the White Sox had come upon hard times in the five years after Baltimore defeated them in the 1983 ALCS. They had posted just one winning record in that span and had also changed managers as Jim Fregosi took over in the middle of the 1986 season for Tony La Russa.

The White Sox would finish the 1988 season with a 71–90 record, fifth place in the AL West. Heading into their series with the Orioles, they were still hovering around .500, trying to stay competitive. After winning five straight, they followed that by losing four of their next six prior to playing the Orioles, entering the series with a record of 10–9.

Former White Sox designated hitter Harold Baines said opposing teams wanted to be done with the Orioles as quickly as possible, not wanting to be the team they beat for their first win. At the same time,

---

1   Chicago actually won one more game than Baltimore during the regular season that year, finishing with a 99–63 record to capture the AL West division title.

he does not recall paying too close attention to the Orioles' struggles at the time, as his own team was trying to right their own ship.

"There is such a day-to-day grind during the baseball season," said Baines, whose major-league career spanned from 1980 to 2001. "You can't get too caught up in the good times or the bad times because there is always another game coming up.

"When you or a team struggles it becomes really easy to press, and players try to win games by themselves all the time," Baines continued. "You have to remember this is a team sport and it takes everyone doing their role, whether it be getting down a bunt, running the bases correctly, or making a play on defense. When that does not happen, teams will lose more often than not."

Taking the mound for the series opener for the White Sox against the Orioles was Jack McDowell. Although McDowell, nicknamed "Black Jack," would go on to be a three-time All-Star and Cy Young Award winner (1993) while winning 127 games over his 12-year career, he was just a twenty-two-year-old rookie in 1988.

The Orioles believed that if they were going to break the losing streak, this game would provide them with the greatest opportunity. Now all they had to do was deliver on the promise Robinson made to Schmidt and Williamson the night before.

The start toward delivering that win began just four batters into the top of the first, when Eddie Murray connected on a two-out, two-run home run to give the Orioles a 2–0 lead. Murray's blast came one batter after Cal Ripken Jr. reached first on a single down the third-base line.

The Orioles would go on to add another run in the top of the fifth before breaking the game open in the seventh when they scored four times off McDowell and reliever John Davis. Those runs would come in a variety of ways, as they had just one hit but took advantage of an error, two walks, and a hit batsman. Billy Ripken was hit in the head by a Davis pitch, and had to be taken off the field in a stretcher. Luckily, Ripken only suffered a mild concussion and X-rays were negative.

"We were lucky it was not worse," Cal Ripken Jr. said in 2017.

With the most runs they'd scored all year, Williamson and Schmidt would do the rest. Just like Robinson said the night before, Williamson, who was mainly a relief pitcher for most of his career, pitched six innings and allowed no runs on three hits while striking out two. Schmidt then took over and pitched three shutout innings, allowing one hit with one strikeout. Neither pitcher walked a batter.

"As I was warming up in the bullpen, [longtime former Orioles bullpen coach] Elrod Hendricks told me it was time to finish the losing streak tonight," Schmidt said. "We wanted nothing more at that point. It was time for it to be over."

Even with the game in control, those on the Orioles roster were not going to take anything for granted until the final out was recorded. Too many things had gone wrong in the young season for them to think otherwise. No one on the team breathed a sigh of relief until Baines, a dangerous hitter who finished his career with 2,866 hits and 384 home runs, grounded out to end the game and put an end to the Orioles' misery.

Many of the 14,059 fans at Comiskey Park even cheered for the visiting team for finally getting a win, the team's first regular-season victory since October 4, 1987. With the victory, the Orioles could at least say they avoided the modern-day major league record twenty-three-game losing streak at any point in the season, which was set by the 1961 Philadelphia Phillies.

"Everyone was nervous until the final out," Ken Rosenthal said. "Even the victory did not come without concerns after Billy Ripken was beaned in the head. He was really lucky he wasn't seriously hurt."

Baines, a native of St. Michaels, Maryland, who would go on to play with the Orioles,[2] said he did not recall much about that game but remembers the historic levels the losing streak reached.

"I don't remember much about that game, other than we were dealing with a lot of our own struggles that season," said Baines, who was elected in the National Baseball Hall of Fame as part of the class of 2019. "I was probably more concerned with trying not to go hitless at the plate that night than worrying about the Orioles losing streak."

Baines, a six-time All-Star who would go on to win a World Series ring as a coach with the White Sox in 2005, said he cannot imagine being on a team that had to deal with such a losing streak and is sympathetic to those who played on the team in 1988.

"Baseball is a streaky sport. You've got to find ways to make adjustments. A losing streak that long is just incredible and so rare. It's still a record today to start a season. That's something no player wants to experience."

Scott Garceau was at Comiskey Park that night. He said as the game got into the later innings and it appeared the Orioles were finally going to win, the ballpark had the feeling of a playoff game. Even with the game in hand, there were those who just would not accept a win until the game had concluded.

"As it appeared the Orioles were finally going to win a game, I made my way down toward the field from the broadcast booth, so I could get player reaction to the end of the streak, which at that point had taken on a life of its own with national media covering the team," Garceau said. "I was not in the dugout but close to it, and you could hear the players starting to get excited.

"It felt like the seventh game of the World Series against the White Sox," Garceau continued. "Dave Schmidt told me after the game that he was shaking and had never been so nervous on the

---

2   Baines played two stints in Baltimore: 1993–1995, and 1999–2000.

mound as he was that night. The Orioles just wanted that streak to be over with and they did not believe anything was certain until they got that final out."

Schmidt said the streak had reached the point where anywhere from fifty to seventy reporters were covering the team on a nightly basis. If anything, Schmidt said he was glad that at least the non-stop national coverage of their losing streak would be over.

"Almost all the reporters covering the team at that point were only interested in following the train wreck that was our season," Schmidt said. "After the game I was asked what I was most glad about with the win. That was easy to answer. I told the reporter that most of you guys would be gone tomorrow except the regular beat reporters because the train wreck was over. I know the Oriole fans were just as frustrated as we were."

In hindsight, Schmidt admits the Orioles were a much more flawed team than he ever realized during that season. He said players are obviously much more optimistic of their chances for success compared to those who are taking a more objective approach to analyzing a team's strengths and weaknesses. Still, even today he believes the losing streak was as freakish as anything he has ever seen or experienced in sports.

"Looking back on that twenty-one-game losing streak, I'm amazed we were not able to pull out at least a game or two," said Schmidt, who posted a 54–55 record in a career that spanned from 1981 to 1992.

"We still had Cal Ripken Jr. and Eddie Murray and Fred Lynn, the latter of which may have been toward the end of his career, but was still putting up good numbers for us," Schmidt continued. "On the pitching side, we had guys with major-league success like Mike Boddicker, Scott McGregor, and myself. We had some good players, but weird things kept happening. It was simply unbelievable at the time and even looking back on it today."

Ripken Jr. said winning a game did take away some stress on the players, but they also understood the daunting task ahead of playing five months of basically meaningless ball.

"When we finally got a win, it felt great to get the monkey off our backs, especially from a media standpoint as the large group of reporters would stop following us on a daily basis," Ripken Jr. said. "It was an abnormal environment, that's for sure. We were still in a position where we had so much of the season still in front of us."

Garceau said the postgame news conference with Frank Robinson was simply surreal. Usually, the interviews with the manager were done in the clubhouse office with a camera or two and a few beat writers. This was definitely not the case.

"There were so many reporters who wanted to cover the end of the losing streak that the press conference had to be done on the field," Garceau said. "There were more media covering that game than those covering a presidential news conference."

As for the rest of the team, there was no celebration; more of just a sense of relief. The moment of relief then switched to a sense of reality: It was April 29, and the Orioles were already 15 1/2 games out of first place in the AL East.

Brooks Robinson said it was tough enough watching the team go through such a losing streak as a member of the broadcast team. He was glad he never had to experience anything close to that as a player over his 23-year career.

"It is hard to imagine a season is lost in the first month like that," Robinson said. "As a competitor you want to keep fighting and not give up. However, a losing streak like that can weigh heavily on any player."

Try to put this losing streak into its proper perspective: the team was fully entrenched in last place in the division with still 140 games to go. Despite such a grim reality, the Orioles, if even for one moment, could catch their breath and appreciate the feeling of a win and go back to simply playing baseball.

"When we finally won a game in Chicago after that 0–21 start, it was a huge sense of relief to finally end the losing," Fred Lynn said. "However, that celebration only lasted a few moments. That is when you have a second to reflect and realize that: it is the end of April, you are 0–21, and your season is basically over before May 1.

"After that win, you look at that record—1–21—and try to figure out what you need to do even to get back to .500 and it is a daunting task. I mean there is still 140 games left to go, and the season is lost," Lynn continued. "At that point you realize just why you have the record you have, and it feels pretty bad."

Other players like Joe Orsulak and Jose Bautista said they were in no mood to celebrate and definitely did not want anything to do with the champagne that may have been in the clubhouse that evening.

"Winning a game was a bittersweet moment for me," Orsulak said. "It was great to finally get a win and end the streak, but it was not something to celebrate, either. It was just time to move on."

Orsulak added that many teams felt bad for what his club was going through. But, at the same time, no one showed them any mercy on the field, either.

"Teams that played us wanted to win three games in a row and get out of town. They did not want to be the first team to lose to us. There is no mercy in professional sports. When a team is down, an opposing team wants to make sure they stay down because a win is a win."

Bautista said the reality of knowing before May 1 that the team would finish in last place (in the division, at least) led him from a sense of relief to a sense of frustration and anguish.

"We had all that champagne in the clubhouse after we finally got that win against the Chicago White Sox, but nobody drank it," Bautista said. "Why would we? We didn't have anything to celebrate. We were a 1–21 team. We were a bad team in last place in the division and out of contention before May 1. That is not something anyone would want to celebrate."

Understanding just how much damage was done to the season in just a few weeks was not lost on anyone.

"It was hard to come to grips that the season was over almost when it started," said retired Orioles trainer Richie Bancells. "Getting that first win did not bring as much joy as it did a sense of relief. However, I know it was tough for the team to be playing out the string so early in that season.

"It's one thing to be playing meaningless baseball in August and September," Bancells continued, "but that hole was just too big to climb out of for any team, let alone one with as many issues as we had in 1988."

Chapter Eight

FANTASTIC FANS NIGHT

The good news for the Orioles was that the losing streak was over. The bad news was the team's season was basically over from a competitive stance just a month into the campaign. All that was left to play for was pride. But in sports, playing for pride is rarely a reason that attracts many fans to the park.

Typically, if a sports team is a winner, the fans will turn out in droves to support the players on the field. However, that was not always the case in Baltimore when it came to the Orioles. Even during the team's glory years, from 1966 to 1983, a full Memorial Stadium was not necessarily the norm. During that span, the Orioles averaged just 1.196 million fans per season. [1]

The high point during that run came in 1983 when they attracted more than two million fans for their final World Series season. During their other World Series title seasons, in 1966 and 1970, the team

---

[1] By comparison, the Dodgers led the majors in attendance with more than 3.5 million fans in 1983 and more than 2.6 million fans in 1966.

attracted 1.203 and 1.057 million fans, respectively. Those figures were good enough to rank third in 1966 and sixth in 1970 for attendance in the American League.

In most cases, during those eighteen seasons, the Orioles ranked in the middle to toward the bottom in average attendance in the AL, including five seasons when they did not even attract a million fans and seven other seasons when they barely reached that attendance threshold.

Fast forward to 1988 and the Orioles were asking fans to come out and support a team who just completed the worst start ever to a baseball season. This was also a season when the team could be considered one of the worst—if not *the* worst—franchises in all of professional sports.

However, there was reason to believe that Baltimore sports fans would still come out and watch their team. In each of the two seasons that followed their last World Series title, the team attracted more than two million fans. Between 1983 and 1985, the Orioles would set attendance records in each season.

There are several factors that played into the jump in attendance. The first came in 1979, the season when "Oriole Magic" was born. It was a season when it seemed that every night a different player stepped up to help propel the Orioles to the pennant.

It was also in August of 1979 that Jerry Hoffberger and his local ownership group sold the franchise to Edward Bennett Williams, a prominent Washington, DC, attorney who at the time was also the president of the NFL's Washington Redskins. Williams's purchase of the Orioles for $12 million was finalized in August 1979, at a time when the team had the best record in baseball and led the AL East by seven games.

Despite all the success on the field, the Orioles were reportedly a money-loser, and the team's financial losses were what eventually led Hoffberger to sell.

Immediately after the sale was finalized, there were concerns that Williams would move the Orioles from Baltimore to Washington. At that point in time, the nation's capital had not had a baseball team since the Washington Senators relocated to Texas and became the Rangers after the 1971 season.

"I did not buy the Baltimore Orioles to move them," Williams told reporters during an August 2, 1979, news conference to announce the sale. "I bought them to play in Baltimore and so long as the people of Baltimore support the Baltimore Orioles, they will stay here. That is my pledge to the city."

That statement by Williams did little to calm the nerves of fans. Williams continued to send mixed signals regarding his intentions early in his ownership. He actually had Larry Lucchino, who would go on to be an executive for the Orioles and later the Boston Red Sox, take a helicopter ride along Interstate 95 to scout out potential stadium sites in Washington, DC.

Such moves would strike fear in many fans, who feared losing another home team to 50 miles south of Baltimore, as the NBA's Bullets had already moved from Baltimore to Landover—a Washington suburb in Maryland—in 1973.

"From the mid-1960s through the early part of the 1970s was a golden age for sports in Baltimore," said Michael Olesker, who also authored the book *The Colts' Baltimore*. "The Colts were still going strong and had won Super Bowl V, the Orioles were winning World Series titles and we even had the Bullets, who while not always the best team in the NBA were one of the most exciting with Earl Monroe and Gus Johnson and Wes Unseld.

"Changes started coming in 1968 after the riots following the death of Dr. Martin Luther King Jr.," Olesker continued. "After the riots, no one wanted to go downtown anymore and that killed the Bullets in town, who eventually moved to Washington."[2]

Over time, those close to Williams said he softened on his thoughts of moving the franchise to Washington, even as he continued to lobby for the need of a new ballpark. At the same time, he worked to bring Washington to Baltimore by signing regional broadcast deals that expanded the Orioles games into other nearby states, removing the Baltimore from the team's road jerseys and heavily marketing them in the Washington market.

Olesker said the concern many fans felt about the possibility of losing their beloved team was real given the ambiguity Williams had when discussing their future with the media.

"Williams never specifically said he would move the team to Washington, but also did little to dispel the concerns," Olesker said. "He said he would stay in Baltimore as long as the fans supported the team, but never provided a number that would represent that support."

The Orioles also received help from the unlikeliest of people to help generate excitement for the team. William Grover Hagy was a cab driver from Dundalk, Maryland. But to those at Memorial Stadium, he was simply known as "Wild Bill" Hagy. Hagy was a lifelong Orioles fan who gained a cult following in the late 1970s after starting the famed "O-R-I-O-L-E-S" chants.

Easily noticed with his bushy beard, straw hat, and sunglasses, Hagy's rally cries, dubbed the "Roar from 34," started in Section 34 of the upper deck of Memorial Stadium, but soon he was found leading the crowd from atop the dugout. Many said Hagy became the

---

2   The Bullets were renamed as the Wizards after the 1996-97 season.

symbol of Oriole Magic, as his cheers often led to come-from-behind victories.

Hagy would become so synonymous with the club that he'd go on to meet presidents Jimmy Carter and Ronald Reagan and would be featured in national media stories. Hagy's relationship with the Orioles became strained by 1985 when he started to boycott Memorial Stadium after he was no longer allowed to bring his own beer cooler into the ballpark. He famously tossed his cooler onto the field and vowed he would never come back.

Hagy did sporadically come back to Orioles games at Oriole Park at Camden Yards in the 1990s, including the night Cal Ripken Jr. broke the record for consecutive games played streak on September 6, 1995. Hagy even performed his O-R-I-O-L-E-S cheer at Ripken's Hall of Fame induction ceremony in 2007. Hagy died just a few weeks later. He was sixty-eight years old.

"While leading cheers from 'The Roar from 34' at Memorial Stadium, Wild Bill became a Baltimore institution," the Orioles said in a statement at the time of Hagy's death. "He was one of the great characters of the Baltimore sports landscape and was a true die-hard Orioles fan, supporting the club year in and year out. He will be missed by everyone who knew him and by everyone for whom he led the 'O-R-I-O-L-E-S' cheer. All of us in the Orioles organization extend our sincere condolences to his family and friends."

* * *

Rallying to support the Orioles and show ownership that Baltimore loved its team also coincided with the fall of the once-great Baltimore Colts franchise. From the late-1950s to mid-1970s, there was no doubt that Baltimore was, first and foremost, a football town. To many fans, it was the Colts who helped put professional football on the national sports landscape in 1958 when they defeated the New York Giants in the NFL Championship Game. The game was dubbed "The Greatest Game Ever Played," as it was the first NFL championship to go into sudden-death overtime.

The Baltimore Colts, led by numerous Hall of Fame greats (quarterback Johnny Unitas, running back Lenny Moore, tight end John Mackey, wide receiver Raymond Berry, and defensive tackle Art Donovan) were to football as the Orioles were to baseball. Fans embraced the Colts' blue-collar mentality and work ethic, following the team as close as any fan base in America. But by the late 1970s, the Colts were in disarray, finishing the 1979 season with a 5–11 record and last place in the AFC East.

Fans also grew tired of the antics and behavior of then-owner Robert Irsay, who ran the once-proud franchise into the ground within a few years after swapping ownership of the Los Angeles Rams with Colts owner Carroll Rosenbloom. Irsay also continued to tug at Baltimore's heartstrings regarding a potential move in part because he wanted the city to build a new stadium (as well as his heart never really being with the city).

Still, no one actually thought Irsay would move the franchise that helped put the NFL on the map. That all changed on March 28, 1984, when he packed up the Colts and moved the team to Indianapolis. The infamous scene of the Mayflower moving vans "sneaking" them out on a snow-filled evening resonates with many Baltimore sports fans to this day. And just like that, Baltimore, which twelve years earlier was home to three professional sports teams, was down to just one.

Baltimore residents, along with elected officials, still heartbroken over losing the Colts—the Ravens would not arrive from Cleveland until 1996—were not going to let the Orioles leave town in a similar fashion. A combination of the team being the only game in town and more fans coming in from neighboring states raised interest and ticket receipts. However, that would only go so far given the team's inability to win during that period.

"There was concern from the time Edward Bennett Williams bought the team that they were moving the team to Washington," said reporter Jeff Seidel. "For many Orioles fans, that fear became greater after the Colts left because they saw how a team could just up and leave in the middle of the night. In the end, though, Williams appeared to be OK with trying to bring Washington fans to the Baltimore Orioles instead of the other way around."

By the mid-to-late 1980s, losing was taking its toll on the gate receipts as attendance dropped precipitously between 1986 and 1988, falling from 1.973 million in 1986 to 1.660 million in 1988.

Olesker chimed in and added that if the mid-1960s to the mid-1970s were the golden age of Baltimore sports, then the mid-to-late 1980s were the dark days in Charm City.

"By 1984, all Baltimore had left was the Orioles and, coincidentally, that was the year they started to falter. It really led to a dark period for sports in Baltimore."

Olesker said the Orioles were just not sure how to adjust to the changing economic realities of sports, especially how it pertained to free agency and the surge of big-time long-term contracts; struggles which played a major role in the franchise's steep decline in just a short period of time.

"Baltimore was always a town that prided itself on the work ethic of its teams, not the money spent on them," Olesker continued. "No one knew how to respond to the changing times. Baltimore was a town with Brooks Robinson, Johnny Unitas, Artie Donovan, and Jim Palmer—athletes who made a career of staying in one place for years. By the 1980s, it was apparent that Baltimore couldn't afford that anymore.

"By 1988, things had gotten really bad for Baltimore as a sports town. The Bullets were long gone. The Colts had just left town and the one team left—the Orioles—had completely fallen apart. I mean 0–21 was historically bad. People in New York wanted to read about it. People all over the world wanted to read about it. Even people in China knew about the losing streak."

With the Orioles mired in their historic losing streak, the front office was looking for ways to show the fans their appreciation for their continued support. This led to the development of "Fantastic Fans Night" on May 2, 1988. The team announced plans for the event around the time of its seventeenth straight loss.

It soon became apparent that the idea was a good one. Quickly, thousands of tickets were sold to the Monday night game against the Texas Rangers. Even more were sold once the Orioles finally won a game.

After getting their first "W" the Orioles would lose their final two games against the Chicago White Sox by scores of 4–1 and 7–3, respectively. So, by the time the "Fantastic Fans Night" arrived, the team had a 1–23 record and were 15 1/2 games out of first place in the AL East.

However, at least on that day, the losses, the uneven play, and the last-place standing meant nothing to those fans in attendance. Local, state, and federal officials also got on board, and about one thousand people gathered at Baltimore's Inner Harbor for a lunch-time rally prior to the game. Then-mayor Kurt Schmoke even proclaimed the day "We Love Our Orioles Day." The hope behind the event was to bring the community together, even if for just one day.

"I think it was important for the fans to come out that first home game after the losing streak ended to show the Orioles they still cared about them," said Schmoke, a Baltimore native who served as mayor from 1987 to 1999. "The fans needed to show the players—and just as importantly the owners—that win or lose, they would support the team. Communities always have divisive issues and sports have always been a way to bring communities together."

Then came the actual game. For those who did not know any better, they would have thought they were attending the seventh game of the World Series and not a Monday night game for a team that was 22 games under .500, as 50,402 people packed Memorial Stadium.

Unbeknownst to those in attendance, the game would take on even more significant meaning just before the first pitch as Maryland Governor William Donald Schaefer, who was in his first term in office, stepped to the microphone during a pregame ceremony. "Stadium agreement reached," Schaeffer said.

What Schaefer was referring to was the agreement of a 15-year lease for the Orioles to play in a soon-to-be downtown baseball-only ballpark which would later become Oriole Park at Camden Yards. The agreement came after a year of negotiations between the Orioles and the Maryland Stadium Authority. The announcement meant even more to Schaefer, who was mayor of Baltimore when the Colts left town and cried when he announced the team was gone. As governor, he was determined not to allow the same thing to happen with the Orioles under his watch.

"We're here because of one man, Edward Bennett Williams," Schaefer told the crowd that night.

Scott Garceau said excitement for the "Fantastic Fans Night" had been growing organically even before the end of the losing streak.

"As we were on the road, word was getting out that thirty-five thousand tickets were sold," said Garceau. "Next we heard forty thousand tickets had been sold and there might even be a sellout. It started to generate a buzz among the players who couldn't believe the fans were still supporting them.

"Many fans had the mindset that, 'The Orioles may be bums,

but they are our bums and we love them no matter what,'" Garceau said. "That Fantastic Fans Night at Memorial Stadium was as unique an event as I have ever covered in my career in Baltimore. I think the fact that the city had just lost the Colts a few years prior played into it. No one wanted to lose another professional sports team in Baltimore. They were going to hold on to the Orioles."

Mike Gibbons shared a similar sentiment. Until everything became official during "Fantastic Fans Night," Gibbons believes many Oriole fans were fearful of seeing moving vans transporting their team out of town just like the Colts had done four years earlier.

"It was a scary time to be a Baltimore sports fan, that is for sure," Gibbons said. "Many people really felt we were going to lose the Orioles just like we had lost the Colts. That would have been devastating for the city. I am just glad it did not come to that."

Olesker agreed. He believes there were many Orioles fans who realized what they were witnessing was a historic event, even if that history was extremely painful for them to endure.

"By 1988, despite the record, the fans had to embrace the Orioles," Olesker said. "It was all the sports the city had. The losing streak had gotten so big, it was beyond disappointing. You just had to sit back and realize you were watching a once-in-a-lifetime event. It became important to remember that baseball is not life or death; it is just a game, and fans had to get beyond the losing streak."

Garceau, who was also the master of ceremonies for the "Fantastic Fans Night" festivities, said he was not made aware of the Oriole Park at Camden Yards announcement until shortly before the fans heard about it in the stadium.

"I was set to MC the program," Garceau said, "but at the last minute, I was told that Governor Schaeffer wanted to make some remarks. He then comes out, points to Edward Bennett Williams in the owner's box, and said that man made sure the Orioles weren't going anywhere and that they would soon be moving into a new stadium in the Camden Yards area of downtown Baltimore.

"The announcement regarding Camden Yards was the lone bright spot in an otherwise horrible season in 1988."

Williams's attendance at the Orioles-Rangers game that night was historic for many reasons. Along with the stadium announcement, it would be the last time he would appear at Memorial Stadium. Williams died three months later, on August 13, 1988, after an eleven-year battle with cancer. He was sixty-eight years old.

"Two things changed in Baltimore that helped keep the Orioles in town," Olesker said. "First, in 1977, Wild Bill Hagy arrived. Before Wild Bill, Baltimore was strictly a Colts town. He made it cool to go to a baseball game and bring a date. Before, the crowds tended to be older and mostly male.

"Also, the radio rights for the Orioles went from WBAL, who did little to promote the team at the time, to WFBR, who promoted the heck out of the team," Olesker continued. "While WFBR did not have the reach of WBAL, they attracted a young audience. That combination helped generate excitement for the Orioles; a franchise who, despite winning, struggled to attract a million fans for years. Then by the end of the 1970s they were setting record crowds, which made it tough for Williams to move the team."

Schmoke, who entered 2019 as the president of the University of Baltimore, was in his first term as Baltimore mayor during the 1988 season. He said that period was a trying time for local sports fans, who had been so used to success for an extended period and nearly lost three major teams in less than two decades.

"There was a lot of dark humor going on at that time wondering if we were ever going to win a game," said Schmoke. "The losing streak took on a life of its own after a while. It was all over the news and being talked about worldwide.

"At the time, there was a lot of uncertainty about sports in Baltimore," Schmoke continued. "The Colts had just left a few years earlier and there was concern that the Orioles could follow them one day. Would the Orioles pack up and move to Washington, or Tampa Bay, or somewhere else?"

With the losing streak in their rear window, the threat of the team moving to Washington or some other city behind them and a new state-of-the-art baseball-only ballpark on the horizon, the players and the fans could breathe a collective sigh of relief. All that was left that night was the game itself.

As the fans chanted O-R-I-O-L-E-S and reminded people why Memorial Stadium was once known as "The World's Largest Outdoor Insane Asylum," the players did their part on the field. Shortstop Cal Ripken Jr. went 2-for-5 at the plate with a home run, an RBI, and three runs scored to lead the Orioles to a 9–4 victory over the Rangers.

Firestone said he remembers being impressed with how the city rallied around the team. He added that there are not too many cities where a show of support like that would occur for a 1–23 baseball team.

"The Orioles fans are as hardcore and loyal as they come," Firestone said. "The attendance was never the best, even when they were winning World Series titles. But those that turned out, guys like Wild Bill Hagy for example, were so passionate about the team and the players."

Keith Mills said while the concept for the "Fantastic Fans Night" was planned, the turnout and reaction by those in attendance was completely organic and something he will not soon forget.

"That crowd on that first home game after the win showed who the true Baltimore sports fans were," Mills said. "It was tough for the

Orioles fans and players to go out to the stadium each night during that season, but they did. That just does not happen with teams that bad."

Ripken's home run in the bottom of the third came after he struck out in the first. During that first at-bat, Ripken received a kiss from Morganna, the so-called kissing bandit. Known for similar stunts from the 1970s through the 1990s, Morganna made her way from the right field stands to kiss Ripken.

"When we got back to that first game at Memorial Stadium and saw all those fans there, it was amazing to see," Fred Lynn said. "Baltimore still loved its baseball team. You've got to remember that back then the Orioles were it in the city. It was a one-sport town at the time.

"That crowd at that game showed us they cared and supported us no matter what," Lynn continued. "I remember talking to my wife after getting traded to Detroit at the end of the season that the crowds in Baltimore were bigger than with the Tigers, and they were competing for a playoff spot. That made me more appreciative of the fans during my time in Baltimore with the Orioles."

Ken Rosenthal said the "Fantastic Fans Night" remains one of his most vivid memories of his long, illustrious career.

"That night was one of the coolest things I've ever seen," Rosenthal said. "I was really amazed with the fans' reaction and how it set the tone for Camden Yards a few years later. The night was the one positive of a truly otherwise forgettable season."

Former Orioles head trainer Richie Bancells said he was floored by the reaction of the crowd on "Fantastic Fans Night." Never in a million years, he said, did he think a sellout crowd would turn out to cheer on a baseball team with just one win a month into the season.

"It was pretty amazing to see the reaction from the fans that night at Memorial Stadium," Bancells said. "We thought everyone would feel the exact opposite. Those were true blue Baltimore Orioles fans there that night. It helped take the sting out of such a horrible season."

The Orioles busted the game open against the Rangers in the bottom of the fourth when they scored five times, which included RBI singles from left fielder Pete Stanicek, second baseman Billy Ripken, and Eddie Murray off Texas starting pitcher Jose Guzman. The Orioles would add three more runs in the bottom of the sixth thanks in part to two bases-loaded walks to right fielder Keith Hughes and catcher Terry Kennedy by Rangers reliever Jose Cecena.

Jay Tibbs would take care of the rest for the home team. He allowed four runs on six hits while striking out seven and walking five in 8 2/3 innings to pick up the win. To those in the stands, the Orioles may have been 2–23 by the end of the game, but they were *their* 2–23 team.

Joe Orsulak said he was touched by how the fans greeted the team that evening and showed him just how great a sports town Baltimore can be—even during the worst of times.

"The reaction and turnout by the fans for that first home game after the win was special," Orsulak said. "If that doesn't prove that the Orioles have the best fans in all of baseball, I don't know what will. They could have just booed us out of the stadium, but they stuck behind us and I don't think most teams can say that about their fans."

Gibbons said many people, including Hall of Fame play-by-play announcer Jon Miller, have called the Fantastic Fans Night their favorite memory involving the Orioles.

"When I have asked Jon Miller about his favorite memories and greatest moments he can recall during his time with the Orioles, it always comes back to that Fantastic Fans Night," said Gibbons.

"Those fans that night would have cheered for anything, even if it was just a squirrel running out onto the field," Gibbons continued. "It just shows just how passionate that Baltimore sports fans can be when it comes to backing their hometown teams."

Ripken Jr. said he was appreciative of how the fans stood by them during such a long losing streak, but admits he was more than ready to put the losing streak behind him by the time "Fantastic Fans Night" came around.

"The Fantastic Fans Night was very uplifting for everyone, but at the same time there was some mixed feeling about it because it brought attention back to a losing streak that we just wanted to go away," Ripken Jr. said. "At the same time, it gave the fans the chance to tell us, 'It's all OK. We're behind you even after such a rough stretch.' In the end, that night proved to be a great starting point to help us move forward and put the losing streak behind us and look toward the future."

Seidel was covering the game that night, speaking with fans to get their thoughts. Among the thousands of games he has covered through the years, he said this game was among the most memorable of his career.

"That first home game after the first win was an amazing experience to witness," Seidel said. "I have been to three World Series games with the Orioles at Memorial Stadium and I don't think any of them had an atmosphere as electric as that game did. The fans just kept getting louder and louder. They were cheering for everything and everybody.

"I think they wanted to show the Orioles that, no matter what, they were going to be there to support their home team," Seidel continued. "The loss of the Colts was still fresh in the minds of so many Baltimore sports fans. There was no way they were going to let the Orioles leave, too, even if the team was horrible.

"Then, to hear that Oriole Park at Camden Yards was going to be built and the team was not going anywhere made the night even more special. The season may have been a lost one but, for one night, the Orioles fans treated their team like World Series champions again."

Chapter Nine

THE FALLOUT

While the emotions surrounding the "Fantastic Fans Night" was great for the players and the fans, it only provided a brief distraction from the fact that the Orioles were at the lowest point of their history. A team that far in last place needed to move in a completely different direction.

Roster turnover had been the norm with the front office the past few seasons. Straying from the "Orioles Way," they were more interested in making trades and taking chances on free agents. Essentially, they were looking for a way—any way—to help return the team to its former glory.

Scott Garceau, who has reported on every major sports story in Baltimore for nearly forty years, said it was obvious the Orioles needed to move in a drastically different direction if it ever wanted to return to a franchise that even closely resembled the one of the mid-1960s to early 1980s.

"At the end of the day, the biggest issue for the Orioles in 1988 was the starting pitching," Garceau said. "It was starting pitching that had always been the strength of the team during their glory years. Yes, they had great hitters like Brooks Robinson and Frank Robinson and Eddie Murray and Cal Ripken, but it was pitching that made the difference. From Jim Palmer and Dave McNally to Scott McGregor and Mike Flanagan to Mike Boddicker and Steve Stone, there were always great pitchers on the Orioles staff. But by 1988, it was literally all gone."

Never one afraid to make a move, Orioles general manager Roland Hemond remained busy throughout the rest of the 1988 season with hopes of righting the ship. Among the first moves was the release of long-time starting pitcher Scott McGregor on May 2, 1988. McGregor spent his entire 13-year career with the Orioles after being traded by the New York Yankees in 1976.

Over the course of his career, McGregor would be one of the most significant pitchers in Orioles history. He was the winning pitcher in the game that clinched the pennant over the California Angels in 1979. In that game, he pitched a complete-game shutout, allowing just six singles while striking out four and walking one in an 8–0 victory.

McGregor was also the winning pitcher for the Orioles in the World Series–clinching victory over the Philadelphia Phillies in 1983. In that game, he pitched another complete-game shutout, allowing just five hits while striking out six and walking two.

McGregor would finish his career with 138 wins and 108 losses, which included a record of 20–8 in 1980. His 107 wins between 1980 and 1988 were among the top ten in the major leagues over that time, trailing such greats as Jack Morris, Fernando Valenzuela, Ron Guidry, and Dave Steib.

But his career began to take a downward trend after he signed a four-year, $4 million contract after the 1985 season; one in which he compiled a 14–14 record. McGregor would never have a winning record again as injuries began to take their toll, as he posted a 13–25 record over his final three seasons. He was 0–3 with an 8.83 ERA at the time of his release. He was actually supposed to start the "Fantastic Fans Night" game, but Hemond informed him of his decision to release him the day before.

McGregor's final start of his career came on April 27, 1988, when he allowed four runs on seven hits, struck out one, and walked one in a loss to the Minnesota Twins. However, McGregor did give the Orioles faithful one brief flashback to his prime years in his final start at Memorial Stadium on April 15, 1988. In that game, McGregor allowed three runs on seven hits, struck out six, and walked three in a 3–2 loss against the Cleveland Indians. The fans gave McGregor a standing ovation as he left the mound in the eighth inning.

"The 1988 roster was full of players who were either on the down-side of their career or were on the major-league roster too early and they may have been successful with more time to develop," Garceau said. "It was a combination of so many things, but the biggest issue was definitely the pitching."

The release of McGregor left Mike Boddicker as the final member of the Orioles 1983 World Series starting rotation to remain with the team. That changed, however, on July 29, 1988, when he was traded to the Boston Red Sox for outfielder Brady Anderson and pitcher Curt Schilling.

The Red Sox felt they were willing to mortgage their future in order to bolster their starting pitching as they were battling the Detroit Tigers for first place in the AL East. The thirty-year-old Boddicker pitched nearly nine seasons with the Orioles and came through with some of the team's most memorable pitching performances. This included winning Game Two in both the Championship Series and World Series in 1983. Both wins came with the Orioles trailing 1–0 in their respective series.

In the 1983 ALCS, Boddicker pitched a complete-game shutout as he allowed just five hits, struck out fourteen, and walked three in a game the Orioles won 4–0 against the Chicago White Sox at Memorial Stadium. Boddicker's performance would garner him the Most Valuable Player Award for the series. In the 1983 World Series, Boddicker again pitched a complete game, allowing just one run on three hits while striking out six and walking none in a game the Orioles won 4–1 over the Phillies.

Boddicker would actually have the best season of his career in 1984 when he posted a 20–11 record with a 2.79 ERA. He made his lone All-Star appearance while leading the AL in wins and ERA.

By 1988, Boddicker was still a solid major league starter. However, like other quality players on the Orioles that season, he struggled early on, losing his first eight decisions with a 5.83 ERA. After his rough start, though, he had a record of 8–4 with a 2.97 ERA in his thirteen starts before the trade. The Red Sox were hoping the Boddicker of late would arrive in Boston.

Being in a pennant race appeared to rejuvenate Boddicker, who posted a record of 7–3 with a 2.63 ERA down the stretch as the Red Sox would win the AL East title before losing to the Oakland Athletics in the ALCS.

In the short term, the trade definitely benefitted the Red Sox. Boddicker would win thirty-nine games for Boston through 1990. During that season, the veteran right-hander would post a 17–8 record with a 3.36 ERA in 228 innings pitched, helping the Red Sox win another American League East title, before losing again to the Athletics in the championship series.

Boddicker would finish his career with a record of 134–116. He spent the 1991 and 1992 seasons with the Kansas City Royals before wrapping up his career with the Milwaukee Brewers in 1993.

Whether the trade was beneficial for the Red Sox in the long term is still up for debate. Boston would have to wait until 2004 before finally winning a World Series title. Could that have happened sooner had they kept Anderson and Schilling? Anderson would go on to spend fourteen of the final fifteen years of his career with the Orioles, where he would develop into one of the best leadoff hitters in the game over that span. For his career, Anderson would hit 210 home runs—including 50 in 1996—and be named an All-Star in 1992, 1996, and 1997. He would also be inducted into the Orioles Hall of Fame before eventually rejoining the team as a member of their front office.

Schilling would go on to develop into one of the best big-game pitchers in baseball history—but that would not happen during his time in Baltimore. The pitcher would spend three lackluster seasons in Baltimore before he, along with pitcher Pete Harnisch and outfielder Steve Finley, were traded to the Houston Astros for power-hitting first baseman Glenn Davis prior to the 1991 season in what is considered the worst deal in Orioles history.

Over the course of his 20-year career, Schilling would post a record of 216–140 with 3,116 strikeouts for the Orioles, Houston Astros, Philadelphia Phillies, Arizona Diamondbacks, and Red Sox. He would also be named to six All-Star teams and win three World Series titles during that span. Ironically, his last two rings came with the Red Sox in 2004 and 2007 after being traded to Boston from the Diamondbacks in November 2003 (where he won a ring in 2001).

The Orioles' purging of their veteran platers continued on August 29, 1988, when they traded utility fielder Jim Dwyer to the Minnesota Twins for a player to be named later.[1] Dwyer was the ultimate role player over his eighteen-year career, which also included

---

1   The Twins would send minor leaguer Doug Kline to the Orioles two days later, completing the trade.

stints with the St. Louis Cardinals, Montreal Expos, Mets (twice), San Francisco Giants, and Red Sox.

Dwyer signed with the Orioles prior to the 1981 season and re-signed with the team twice over the next seven seasons prior to the trade. His best season in Baltimore came in 1983, when he batted .286 with eight home runs, 38 RBIs, and 37 runs scored in 100 games played. (He was batting just .226 in limited playing time before the trade to the Twins.) Dwyer would play for both the Twins and Expos before retiring after the 1990 season. He then transitioned to managing and coaching in the minor leagues before finally retiring in 2017 after spending eleven seasons as the hitting coach of the Fort Myers Miracle, a Single-A affiliate of the Twins.

After the Dwyer deal, outfielder Fred Lynn would be the next veteran to be dealt. His trade to the Tigers—two days after the Dwyer deal—on August 31, 1988, became one of the most unique transactions in baseball history. First, Lynn had to waive the no-trade clause. He reportedly wanted another year tacked onto his deal, which went through 1989. In the end he waived the no-trade clause for a reported $250,000 bonus.

Lynn then took a chartered jet flight from Ontario, California to meet the Tigers in Chicago. This is where the deal got interesting. Lynn said he had to drive 25 miles from Anaheim to Ontario and got delayed due to rush hour traffic. The flight was supposed to reach Chicago's O'Hare Airport at about 12 a.m. central time. However, the pilot could not contact the O'Hare tower until about 12:10 a.m. and did not land the plane until 12:30 a.m.

The reason this is important is because, based on MLB rules at the time, a player had to report to his new club by midnight local time on August 31 to qualify for the team's postseason roster. But, if the player was traveling by airplane to join his new team, the pilot must at least make contact with the tower by midnight on that date. There was significant debate as to whether Lynn would be able to play in the postseason due to this delay.

The debate ended up being moot as the Tigers lost their first six games and ten of eleven after acquiring Lynn. They went on to lose seventeen of their final twenty-seven games and finished one game behind the Red Sox in the AL East. Lynn batted .222 with seven home runs and 19 RBIs during that month. He played one more season with the Tigers and an additional season after that with the San Diego Padres before retiring at the end of the 1990 season.

"When I got traded, it was like a shot in the arm for me on the field," said Lynn, who now lives in San Diego, California. "I had a great September and my love for the game was reignited after going from the worst team in baseball to a playoff contender."

The trade of Lynn ended the tenure of one of the more frustrating signings in Orioles history. Lynn represented the biggest name the team signed in free agency in the years immediately following their World Series victory in 1983. Lynn would hit 23 home runs in each of the three full seasons he played in Baltimore. In 1985, his first full season with the club, he led the majors with six ninth-inning home runs, including three that led to walk-off victories. At the same time, Lynn remained injury-prone and missed more than 150 games during his three-plus seasons in Baltimore. The most games Lynn played with the Orioles in one season was 124 in 1985.

The Lynn trade to the Tigers was a deal that definitely went in the Orioles' favor. In return, Baltimore received catching prospect Chris Hoiles, who would go on to be the team's primary catcher for much of the next decade before retiring after the 1998 season. Hoiles would hit 151 home runs in his career, including a walk-off grand slam on a full count with two outs in the bottom of the ninth to lead the Orioles to a win over the Seattle Mariners on May 17, 1996.

The final major trade was the biggest for the club and took place after the season when they dealt long-time power hitting first baseman Eddie Murray to the Los Angeles Dodgers. The deal was finalized on December 4, 1988, with the Orioles acquiring shortstop prospect Juan Bell, relief pitcher Brian Holton, and starting pitcher Ken Howell.

At the time of the trade, Murray was the most-tenured player on the team. Over his twelve years in Baltimore, Murray batted .295 with 333 home runs and 1,190 RBIs. In his final season before being traded, Murray, who was thirty-two at the time, batted .284 with 28 home runs and 84 RBIs. While Steady Eddie is among the most revered players in franchise history, he often had an uneven relationship with the local media and was ready to move on by the end of the 1988 season. The Dodgers appeared to be the perfect move for Murray, who was going from a last place team to the defending World Series champions. He was also a Los Angeles native, so was happy to be playing in his hometown for the first time in his Hall of Fame career.

The parameters of the deal were developed during the winter meetings in Atlanta, Georgia. Both teams were set to announce the trade during a news conference, which ended up being delayed by about 45 minutes when the general managers, managers, and other key personnel from the clubs got trapped in an elevator between the tenth and eleventh floors of the Marriott Marquis.

Those in the front office also agreed that it was time to move Murray, as they wanted to get rid of his contract. The future Hall of Famer should have provided the team with the perfect trading piece to help facilitate their rebuilding process. However, much like the Glenn Davis trade a few years later, the Murray deal is one that still frustrates many Orioles fans to this day.

"It was a shame how the Eddie Murray deal played out during that offseason," said Baltimore sports historian Mike Gibbons. "The internal squabbling within the front office and ownership affected their relationship with Murray and their ability to get the best deal possible. Eddie was as popular as they came in the clubhouse and among the fans.

"However, Eddie was never one who really liked to speak with the media and that affected his perception among those who covered him," Gibbons continued. "I think that perception made its way into the front office and led the team to trade him. The players the Orioles got back in return did not make it a good trade for the team."

None of the players the Orioles acquired in the Murray deal would go on to have much, if any, impact on the team—or anywhere else in baseball for that matter. The centerpiece was supposed to be Bell, the younger brother of former power hitting outfielder George Bell. The younger Bell was just twenty years old at the time of the trade and considered a top prospect from the time the Dodgers signed him when he was just sixteen years old. The original plan was for Cal Ripken Jr. to eventually move from shortstop to third base to make room for Bell.

But that never happened.

Bell saw limited time as a September call-up in 1989, and even fewer appearances in 1990 as he played in just thirteen games with six at-bats. Bell was finally given an opportunity in 1991, mostly appearing as a pinch hitter and splitting time with Billy Ripken at second base. Unfortunately for Bell, his promise on the field never materialized. In his only full season in Baltimore, Bell batted just .172 with one home run and 15 RBIs. On August 11, 1992, Bell was traded to the Phillies, and was selected off waivers by the Milwaukee Brewers in June of 1993. After being released by the Brewers, he would go on to play for the Montreal Expos and Boston Red Sox along with various minor league teams and even in the Mexican League before retiring in 2000. Bell passed away from kidney disease on August 24,

2016, in Santo Domingo, Dominican Republic. He was just forty-eight years old.

Holton was at least an established major-league pitcher when arriving in Baltimore. The right-hander came up with the Dodgers in 1985, was a member of the team's bullpen in their championship season, recorded a save in Game Five of the NLCS against the Mets and was a clutch reliever against the Athletics in the World Series in 1988.

Holton managed to stick around Baltimore for the 1989 and 1990 seasons and pitched mostly out of the bullpen, although he did make 12 starts in his first season with the club. He finished his major-league career in 1990 with a lifetime record of 20–19, a 3.62 ERA, and 210 strikeouts. Reportedly, Holton never emotionally recovered from being traded by the Dodgers and struggled with substance abuse after officially retiring from baseball in 1992, ending up in jail and was even periodically homeless.

As for Howell, he never suited up for the Orioles, being traded four days later to the Philadelphia Phillies for outfielder Phil Bradley. Bradley would end up being the best acquisition for the Orioles associated in some way with the Murray trade, batting .277 and .256 in 1989 and 1990, respectively, and driving in 86 runs while stealing 37 bases combined over that span.

The Orioles would eventually trade Bradley midway through the 1990 season to the Chicago White Sox for left fielder/designated hitter Ron Kittle. Bradley then played with the Yomiuri Giants in Japan in 1991 before retiring.

"At least at that point, the team finally understood it needed to rebuild and started to move some of the veteran players along," Ripken Jr. said. "We got some good young players during that time, including Brady [Anderson] in the trade for Boddicker and the trade of Mike Morgan to the Dodgers, which brought us Mike Deveraux early in 1989.

"Those trades gave us an exciting outfield for several years and they were fun to watch play during that period," Ripken continued. "Having outfielders like that allows pitchers to throw strikes because they know the fielders behind them will get to the balls hit toward their direction."

Chapter Ten

YOUTH MOVEMENT

With a last-place finish guaranteed and several of the team's older veterans—along with most of the remnants of the 1983 World Series team—traded or released, the Orioles now had the opportunity to use the rest of the 1988 season to attempt to rebuild with younger, up-and-coming, and in many cases untested players.

This started with the starting pitching, which was now without Mike Boddicker and Scott McGregor, who had anchored the staff for much of the 1980s. The first beneficiary of the loss of Boddicker and McGregor was Jeff Ballard, a left-hander who was selected by the Orioles in the seventh round of the 1985 MLB June Amateur Draft out of Stanford University.

At one point, Ballard was considered the organization's top pitching prospect and received his first shot in the majors in 1987. He won his first two decisions after being called up from Triple-A Rochester in May, pitching at least seven innings in each start. However, he would go on to lose his final eight decisions, including five after being called up from the minors in September. However, he struggled the rest of the way and was eventually sent back down to the minors.

Ballard was then given the chance to make the pitching staff out of spring training in 1988, but was sent to minor-league camp in late March. He admits that was the right call for him at that point in his career.

"It was probably the best for me not to be on the team during that stretch of the losing streak," Ballard said. "Being a young pitcher, it was a great opportunity to have the chance to pitch regularly and experience success at the Triple-A level in Rochester. I really needed to be on a good team to be successful at that time.

"The 1988 season obviously went downhill fast," Ballard continued. "From the 12–0 loss on Opening Day to Cal Sr. getting fired after six games to the 21-game losing streak, it was a lost season for sure."

Ballard worked his way back to the majors as the Orioles recalled him on May 21, 1988, and he made the most of that opportunity. In his season debut, he allowed one run on ten hits, struck out three, and walked none in 8 1/3 innings against the Seattle Mariners, with the club winning 3–1.

After allowing six runs (two earned) over five innings in a 7–2 loss to the Milwaukee Brewers on August 7, Ballard had a record of 5–10. He said his confidence was at an all-time low and was unsure what his future held as a professional ballplayer. He was also unsure how to approach the issue, and believed that reaching out to manager Frank Robinson, who could be an imposing figure, was a daunting task at the time.

"I was a pouty kid early on, but [former Orioles first base coach and later manager] Johnny Oates talked to me and turned my attitude around," Ballard said.

In the end, Ballard did not need to broach the subject with Robinson. The manager made his intentions known when speaking to a reporter around this time.

"One day I saw Frank quoted in a newspaper article where he said that 'Ballard isn't going anywhere. He accomplished all he needed to in Triple-A. He will either learn to do it here or he won't,'" Ballard said. "That assurance that I was up to stay was all I needed. The next game out, which was August 13 and my birthday—I'll never forget—I pitched a complete-game shutout against the Brewers. That really helped set the stage for me in 1989."

In that game, the youngster allowed just three hits, walked seven, and struck out one as the Orioles defeated the Brewers, 5–0. Ballard was nearly as good in his next start on August 18, when he allowed a run on four hits, struck out three, and walked five in a complete-game effort against the Oakland A's that the Orioles won 10–1. Despite pitching in the minors for more than a month at the start of the season, Ballard would go on to lead the Orioles in wins with eight, an obvious sign of just how difficult the season was for Baltimore.

"I led the team in wins that season, but it did not come without struggles," said Ballard, who would strike out 41 batters and walk 42 in 153 1/3 innings. "I had a rough stretch in July and thought for sure that I was heading down to Rochester after each start. But I kept getting the call every fifth day. I wasn't sure where I stood with Frank at the time and that put added pressure on me."

* * *

A vital piece of the bullpen would arrive in September 1988 in closer Gregg Olson. Olson was just twenty-one years old when the Orioles drafted him as the fourth overall player in the 1988 MLB June

Amateur Draft out of Auburn University. During his three-year stay at Auburn, Olson compiled a 25–7 record with 20 saves and a 3.03 ERA while striking out 271. A *Baseball America* All-American in 1987 and an ABCA and *Baseball America* selection in 1988, Olson was also a 1987 USA National Team member when he led the NCAA with a 1.26 ERA. In 1988, he led the Southeastern Conference with a 2.00 ERA.

Olson appeared in just 16 minor-league games—appearing in eight for both Single-A Hagerstown and Double-A Charlotte—before being called up in September. He appeared in ten games that season, posting a record of 1–1 with nine strikeouts and ten walks in 11 innings pitched. Olson showed flashes of his future potential in his first major-league appearance on September 2, against the Seattle Mariners at the old Kingdome.

With the Orioles trailing 3–1, Olson replaced starter Mark Thurmond after he had allowed a lead-off single to first baseman Alvin Davis in the bottom of the eighth. After getting designated hitter Steve Balboni to strike out looking, Olson allowed a single to catcher Scott Bradley. Bradley was tagged out at second trying to stretch a single into a double, but Davis advanced to third on the play. Olson followed that by walking right fielder Jay Buhner before getting third baseman Jim Presley to strike out looking to end the threat.

Holding the Mariners in check that inning was huge, as the Orioles rallied to score three times with two out in the top of the ninth thanks to a two-run single by Pete Stanicek off reliever Mike Schooler and an RBI single by Joe Orsulak off Bill Wilkinson. Orioles closer Tom Nidenfuer then came in for the bottom of the ninth to shut down the Mariners and earn the save in Baltimore's 4–3 victory.

Olson said that his rookie contract guaranteed him a September call-up. While he was thankful for the major-league experience so early in his career, he admits some uncertainty joining a team that had played so poorly over the course of the past several years, especially in 1988.

"I was not sure what to expect with the Orioles when I got drafted out of college," Olson said. "At the time, I was hoping to go to the Los Angeles Dodgers or another team on the West Coast. I was glad to get that taste of major-league hitters as a September call-up. It gave me the confidence to know I could get big-league hitters out on a regular basis."

Olson showed the Orioles enough in those final weeks of the season to convince the club to hand the closer role over to him heading into 1989. With Don Aase and Tom Niedenfuer no longer in the team's plans, the closer job was Olson's to lose. Teammates said his presence in the backend of the bullpen made other relievers on the team much better for years to follow.

Orsulak said Olson provided a stabilizing force in the team's bullpen. He called the reliever a vital cog in their success during his tenure with the team between 1988 and 1993.

"One of the big differences in the 1989 team was the addition of Gregg Olson as the closer," Orsulak said. "Part of winning baseball is having a pitcher that can close out a game. We didn't have that in 1988 and it cost us several games during that [losing] streak. We knew once Gregg took the mound, he was bringing that curveball and the game was over. We do not succeed in 1989 without his contributions [as the closer]."

The Orioles also used the lost season to offer their young position players a chance to prove their worth at the major-league level. Catcher Mickey Tettleton would be another player who would receive an extended look over the final weeks and months of the season. Five years younger than opening-day starter Terry Kennedy, Tettleton appeared in 86 games for the Orioles in 1988, batting .261 with 11 home runs and 37 RBIs.

Outfielder Brady Anderson gave the Orioles an infusion of speed and youth that they desperately needed in the field while addressing an area which observers said was one of the more glaring weaknesses heading into the season. Then just twenty-four years old, Anderson played in most of his games as the team's center fielder after being traded from the Red Sox, appearing in 53 games while batting .198 with eight doubles, nine RBIs, and six stolen bases.

Craig Worthington was the latest Oriole who attempted to be the player the team hoped could carry on the standard of play at third base set by Hall of Famer Brooks Robinson. After Robinson retired in 1977, the Orioles tried several different players to fill that void with varying degrees of success. Players like Doug DeCinces, Todd Cruz, and Rick Schu each tried to lay claim to the position, but none proved to be the long-term answer. In between, Cal Ripken Jr. started and ended his career at third base but was moved to shortstop on July 1, 1982.

Worthington appeared in nine games for the Orioles early in the season but played mostly for Triple-A Rochester before being a September call-up when the team rosters expanded. Worthington received an extended look during the final weeks of the season, batting .186 with two home runs and four RBIs in 26 games. Despite the limited success, the Orioles were willing to turn the position over to him heading into the 1989 season. Being the team's first-round pick in 1985, the hope was that he would improve his play the following season.

* * *

Despite all the trades, releases, roster moves, and September call-ups, the season ended with nearly as much frustration as it began. The Orioles lost 21 of their final 28 games before mercifully ending the year with a 9–3 loss at the Toronto Blue Jays on October 2. The end result was a 54–107 record, a last-place finish in the AL East and 34 1/2 games behind the first-place Boston Red Sox.

Jose Bautista said it felt good to put that season to rest, take some time off to refocus during the offseason, and try to look toward the following Spring Training.

"It was really a rough season for me being a rookie," Bautista said. "Had I been on a better team with some better offense and defense, I could have won 15 games, not lost that many based on my stats that year compared to pitchers on other teams in the league."

Joe Orsulak said the final several months of that season offered many players a chance to show they belonged in the major leagues, either with the Orioles or some other team. In other words, while team goals were out of reach, plenty of players had individual motivations to keep playing hard—especially for younger players.

"It was obvious we were not going to be competing for the pennant in 1988," Orsulak said. "But there was still so much for a player to play for. Personally, I was playing for my career. I usually did not have the luxury of playing on a multi-year contract. I was year to year for much of my career. That season was no exception.

"How I played that year determined whether I was going to stay in the majors," Orsulak continued. "There is only so much an individual player can do on a baseball team. But it is up to each player to continue to compete. You have to remember this is your job and try to find a way to contribute to a win each time out on the field. You can't worry about the standings when your career is on the line."

Plenty more changes would be needed if the Orioles were to be competitive in 1989, a season which would turn out to be one of the most memorable in Baltimore and arguably one of the most unlikely in MLB history.

Chapter Eleven

WHY NOT?

The Orioles entered the 1989 season determined to put 1988 as far in the rearview mirror as possible. The year was to be one of rebirth and revival. The transition actually began on December 8, when New York businessman Eli Jacobs, along with Orioles executive Larry Lucchino and Sargent Shriver—the brother-in-law of President John F. Kennedy—purchased the Orioles for $70 million from the estate of Edward Bennett Williams.

Then, with general manager Roland Hemond in his second full year at the helm and Frank Robinson fully entrenched as the team's manager, the Orioles were ready for a fresh start with a significantly retooled roster.

More than half the roster—including seven members of the Opening Day starting lineup—were different than just a year prior. Entering the 1989 season, Cal Ripken Jr. was the only player remaining on the roster from the 1983 World Series team. The wheeling and dealing of players continued into Spring Training, when the team traded starting pitcher Mike Morgan to the Los Angeles Dodgers for up-and-coming outfielder Mike Devereaux.

Much like the Eddie Murray trade a few months earlier, this move provided a young player an opportunity to make a major-league club while offering a veteran player the chance to move from a last-place team to the defending World Series champions. But unlike shortstop Juan Bell, Devereaux would prove to be a valuable player in Baltimore for several seasons, including his first year with the club.

The club had valued Devereaux for several months, and there was even discussion of him being included in the Murray deal. Instead, Devereaux was sent to Baltimore for a pitcher who, up to that point, had a lifetime record of 34–68 with an ERA of 4.90. In 1988, he had a 1–6 record with an ERA of 5.43.

The ceiling remained much higher on Devereaux, who was just twenty-five years old at the time of the trade. Once considered a prospect for the Dodgers, Devereaux hit just .222 and .116 in limited opportunities for Los Angeles the previous two seasons. The Dodgers believed that with Mike Marshal, Kirk Gibson, and John Shelby as starters, and reserves like Mike Davis and Franklin Stubbs also available for play in the outfield, Devereaux was expendable.

"The awful year we had in 1988 forced the Orioles to make changes, and many of the moves they made laid the foundation for the success we had in 1989," Jeff Ballard said.

Originally a fifth-round choice in the 1985 MLB June Amateur Draft out of Arizona State, Devereaux was ready to go anywhere if it meant he would be given an opportunity to succeed on the major-league level.

While nervous about moving from the defending World Series champions to the worst team in baseball, the young outfielder was simply happy to be in camp with the expectation that he would be done playing in the minors.

"I knew the Orioles had lost twenty-one games in a row to start the previous season, but I didn't know much more about the team at that time," said Devereaux. "I was young and did not really understand all the intricacies involved with trades and what to expect as the season approached. I just knew that the Orioles had been interested in me and I was not sure if the same opportunity to play every day was going to be there with the Dodgers, who had a logjam in the outfield. I was also excited to know that I would get the chance to play with a great player like Cal Ripken Jr. From that perspective I was excited to see what Baltimore had to offer."

In the end, Devereaux was just happy to play and was not going to let the team's previous season put a damper on his expectations for a successful year and future.

"There were a lot of questions when I joined the Orioles about my feelings of going from first to worst in the standings. I just remember telling people that we are just in Spring Training right now and we have a long way to go before the regular season even gets started. Let's withhold judgement on the Orioles until we start playing games that really matter."

Even with much of last season's roster jettisoned, fans' expectations for the club remained low. Those with the organization were not sure what to expect, with the only hopes being that the team would at least be somewhat more competitive. In reality, with the exception of Ripken Jr., the Orioles were a team of unknowns—even to the most passionate supporters.

The most immediate concern going into 1989 was to avoid an extended losing streak to start the season. However, Baltimore would not be dealt a good hand on Opening Day as they hosted the defending AL East champion Boston Red Sox before an announced crowd of 52,161 fans on April 3, 1989.

Compounding the issues on Opening Day was the fact that the

Red Sox were sending ace pitcher Roger Clemens to the mound. Clemens, who would go on to win 354 games and seven Cy Young awards over a 24-year career, had gone 18–12 while leading all of baseball with 291 strikeouts the previous season.

"It was a good thing we had a lot of new players on the team in 1989 because for them the losing streak was a non-factor," Joe Orsulak said. "They did not have that experience and those that did were motivated to make sure it did not happen again."

On paper, the Orioles should have lost 12–0 like they had to the Milwaukee Brewers the year before. Instead, they actually jumped out to an early lead in the bottom of the fourth. Brady Anderson led off the inning with a walk and later stole second base. Two batters later, Orsulak lined a single to center field to drive in Anderson and give the Orioles a 1–0 lead.

Devereaux said there were many who spoke to him before the game that said just getting a hit off Clemens on Opening Day would be considered a victory.

"Can you believe that?" Devereaux said. "We had not even played one game yet and people thought we were so bad that we would not even get a hit on Opening Day. Even then, I knew how good Roger Clemens was, but I did not think it was right for us to be that disrespected just as the season started. We were not the 1988 Orioles. We were our own team full of new, young players ready to make their own statement on the field."

The Red Sox responded by scoring three runs in the top of the sixth off starter Dave Schmidt. Future Hall of Fame third baseman Wade Boggs led off the inning with a double. After a sacrifice by second baseman Marty Barrett, moving Boggs to third, right fielder Dwight Evans—who would play for the Orioles two years later—drove in Boggs with a double to tie the game. Left fielder Mike

Greenwell came up next and hit a two-run homer to deep right-center to give the Red Sox a 3–1 lead.

That could have been the game. In 1988, it probably was the game. But this wasn't 1988. And so, the boys from Baltimore showed their resiliency when they rallied back to score three runs of their own in the bottom of the inning, thanks to a three-run homer by Ripken, giving them a 4–3 lead. That lead was short-lived, however, as short-stop Jody Reed connected with a one-out RBI single off Schmidt in the top of the seventh to tie the game at four. It was the last batter Schmidt would face.

Unlike the previous year, the Orioles did not make a crucial error in the field, a base running mistake, or some other miscue to cost them the game. Instead, their bullpen came in and did not allow a run in the final 4 2/3 innings. This included 4 1/3 from Brian Holton, who allowed three hits, walked two, and struck out two.

The game remained tied at four until the bottom of the 11th. With Bob Stanley on the mound, Mickey Tettleton reached first on a one-out walk. Pinch hitter Randy Milligan then singled to right field to advance Tettleton to third. With Mike Smithson replacing Stanley on the mound, Craig Worthington connected on a single to left-center that drove in Tettleton and gave the Orioles a 5–4 walk-off victory in front of the raucous, pleasantly shocked home crowd. With that base hit, the Orioles were officially able to end any talk of a repeat to the disastrous 1988 season.

"Just like Opening Day set the tone in 1988, the same could be said about the 1989 season," Ballard said. "When you beat Roger Clemens and the Red Sox, you feel like you can do anything. It all just snowballed from there. There was energy and excitement on the team that was not there the year before."

Orsulak said getting a win over the defending divisional

champions helped relax the team, who were obviously worried about struggling in 1989 much like they had the year before.

"Opening Day in 1989 was so important to the players on the team, especially those that went through the losing streak in 1988," said Orsulak, who went 1-for-4 at the plate with an RBI in the win over the Red Sox. "When you start a season losing 21 games in a row, winning on Opening Day becomes so important. Beating the Red Sox and Roger Clemens that day was just uplifting for the whole team."

That was exactly how pitcher Jose Bautista felt. He said winning on Opening Day was the perfect way for the team to put the 1988 season in the rearview mirror. He added that a big difference from one season to the next was team chemistry and just how much better the group meshed compared to the previous season.

"The key for us was to start the season the right way and win early so any talk about the losing streak would end," Bautista said. "We were able to do that right from Opening Day."

"They made a lot of the right moves entering the 1989 season," Bautista continued. "We came out in Spring Training with the hope of putting 1988 behind us and doing our best to improve in 1989. That is exactly what we were able to do from Day One."

Devereaux said he felt Ripken's home run helped provide the energy and confidence they needed to compete against a pitcher the caliber of Clemens and a team the caliber of the Red Sox.

"Cal set the tone for the rest of the team in that game," Devereaux said. "We had I think the youngest team in the American League at that point and really wanted to show the rest of baseball that we were a new team and not the Orioles of old."

They also happened to be playing in an AL East which was far from the powerhouse conference baseball fans today are accustomed to.

* * *

After defeating the Sox on Opening Day and again three days later, the team hovered around .500 for the first few weeks of the season. By May 21, they had a record of 18–21 following a 2–0 loss against the Cleveland Indians at Memorial Stadium.

Then something began to click.

In the first game of a six-game road trip against the White Sox and Indians, on May 22, the Orioles won 5–1 with some of their new, young talent leading the way. An RBI triple by Devereaux in the fourth and a home run by Anderson in the seventh helped rejuvenate the team not only in that game but moving forward that season.

"We did not know any better," said Devereaux, who would bat .266 with eight home runs, 46 RBIs, 22 stolen bases, and 55 runs scored in 122 games in 1989. "We were just playing hard and having a lot of fun. It was really turning into an awesome rookie year for me."

The Orioles would go on to win the first five games of the road trip and 13 of 14 overall. By the time they routed the New York Yankees, 16–3, on June 5 at Yankee Stadium, the team's record reached 31–22 and they had a five-game lead in the AL East. By comparison, the Orioles did not win their 31st game of the season in 1988 until July 23.

Closer Gregg Olson said the "Why Not?" season was just one where all the breaks went Baltimore's way, and balls that bounced one way in 1988 bounced in a completely different direction the following season.

"That win on Opening Day was a nice way to get the season going and gave us some confidence but, in the end, it was just one game out of 162," said Olson, who would eventually save 217 games over the course of his 14-year career.

"I don't think there was a light switch that turned on for us," Olson continued. "It was just the whole season for the team. I think the world started to take us seriously by the All-Star break when they saw we were at the top of the standings. Other than Cal Ripken, we were a bunch of unknowns who did not know we were not supposed to be in last place."

Keith Mills said even though it took the Orioles a few weeks to get going, the combination of winning on Opening Day and a roster full of young, energetic players helped the team forget that they were not expected to be contenders.

"That Opening Day in 1989 was so important to the fans and the players," Mills said. "Get a win that day and the talk of 1988 would go away. That is exactly what happened, and it set the stage for one of the most special seasons in Orioles history. Had there been a wild card in place that season, who knows what the Orioles could have accomplished. The way they played against the Oakland A's that year, they may have gotten back to the World Series. All the egos were set aside on that team for the greater good of trying to win the division."

The team's rebuilding efforts were coming to fruition quicker than the franchise—or anyone else—could have imagined. This was no more apparent than the emergence of Ballard as the ace of the pitching staff. In the win against the Yankees, Ballard allowed two runs on nine hits while striking out three and walking six to win his fifth-straight decision, improving his record to 9–1 with a 2.12 ERA.

What made Ballard's run even more impressive was that he often picked up a win while going up against the other team's best pitcher. This included defeating Frank Viola and the Minnesota Twins on April 9, Mike Boddicker and the Boston Red Sox on April 15, Brett Saberhagen and the Kansas City Royals on April 20, and Dave Stewart and the Oakland A's on May 11.

Ballard said the opportunity he received at the end of the 1988 season really helped put him in a positive mindset moving forward.

"We played with confidence and many of us were just too young and stupid to realize we were playing over our heads," Ballard said. "It was a special season, that is for sure, and one that I know is a favorite for many Orioles fans who grew up during that time."

Other players who came through with breakout seasons in 1989 included Tettleton and Worthington. Tettleton was a player that was easy for the Orioles' blue-collar fan base to embrace. A former journeyman catcher, Tettleton was also an offensive catalyst on the roster.

Tettleton's tenure in Baltimore was relatively short, but his legend continues to grow. Known for his huge arms and a batting stance all his own, Tettleton belted a team-high 26 home runs, made the All-Star team, and carried the offense for much of the season.

Adding to his lore, Tettleton will be remembered for his love of the children's cereal Fruit Loops, as he was known for eating the sugary cereal every day as one of his superstitions. The love of Fruit Loops caught on with fans, who would throw the cereal like confetti after Tettleton homered. Fans would also shout "Loops" when Tettleton came to the plate and even brought boxes of the cereal to the stadium for him to autograph.

Worthington used the September 1988 call-up as a springboard for a great 1989 season. Just twenty-four years old, Worthington played in 145 games and batted .247 with 15 home runs and 70 RBIs on the way to being named *The Sporting News* American League Rookie of the Year.

With a roster filled mostly with retreads, unknowns, and rookies, the Orioles entered the All-Star break with a record of 48–37 and led the AL East by 5 1/2 games. The team's run toward their first divisional title in six years seemed to improve after the break, as they won five of their first six games, including two walk-offs, extending their lead to 7 1/2 games after a 4–3 victory against the Seattle Mariners on July 18.

Orsulak admits that the 1989 team overachieved that season. The wins just kept coming and players were determined to enjoy the ride for as long as it lasted while trying to make baseball history in the process.

"Whatever the reason, the players on that 1989 team were fearless and not intimidated by the competition," Orsulak said. "Many teams were intimidated by the A's that year with players like Mark McGwire, Jose Canseco, and Ricky Henderson on the roster. Some teams were defeated before ever stepping onto the field.

"Players who faced adversity like we did in 1988 just needed to go out there and do their job the next season," Orsulak continued. "You can't be worried about what others are doing because it's out of your control. When you try to do too much, it can often make things worse. Everyone was just trying to do their part in 1989."

However, the Orioles magic that carried the team for so many months began to fade. Baltimore would lose their next eight games and 13 of 14 contests to fall to 54–51 after a 6–2 loss at the Red Sox on August 1. Their division lead was now down to a single game, with the Red Sox and Blue Jays nipping at their tail.

Still, the Orioles continued to weather the storm. The team posted an 18–13 record in August that included winning streaks of three and four (twice) games in a row at various points over the month. At the same time, the Blue Jays began to heat up and won 11 of their final 13 games in August to pull even with the Orioles, setting the stage for a dramatic and competitive final month of the season.

While Ballard and Tettleton made the difference in the early stages of the season, different role players continued to come through with big individual efforts down the stretch to keep the team in contention. Orsulak said getting big plays in spurts from various players helped keep them in contention.

"That season, we had a bunch of starting pitchers that no one had ever heard of before who stepped up big time," Orsulak said. "Jeff Ballard? Bob Milacki? Pete Harnisch? Dave Johnson, a thirty-year-old rookie? None of them had a track record of success in the big leagues up to that point.

"Jeff Ballard in spring training in 1988 and 1989 was one of the most horrible pitchers out there. He could not get anyone out and I was wondering what we would get out of him." Orsulak continued. "But then, the season got started in 1989 and he got on a roll like no other pitcher in baseball that season. It just gave the whole team confidence."

Roy Firestone said the 1989 team had a completely different vibe and aura resonating from them compared to the same group one year before. The uniforms were the same and they played in the same stadium, but there was no denying the heart the 1989 club played with. It was the story of the ultimate underdog and a team that, for at least one season, captured the hearts and minds of baseball fans across the country. Fans were rooting for them to not only pull off arguably the greatest turnaround in baseball, but in professional sports history.

"The following year was completely different for so many reasons." Firestone said. "It was a season where quality trades, signings, and player development came together at the same time and paid some dividends.

"The pitching was so much better, too," Firestone continued. "Jeff Ballard had a career year and guys like Bob Milacki, Dave Schmidt, Pete Harnisch, and Dave Johnson came up huge in the rotation. Then you had a shutdown bullpen with a shutdown closer in Gregg Olson coming up big as well."

Among those role players that came up big for the team during the "Why Not?" season was starting pitcher Dave Johnson.

Johnson, no relation to the former Orioles second baseman and manager with the same name, grew up in Middle River, Maryland; a working-class community in the Baltimore suburbs. He was the definition of a journeyman, having spent seven seasons in the minors with the Pittsburgh Pirates and Houston Astros organizations before being acquired by the Orioles during Spring Training. Johnson, who started the season with Triple-A Rochester, was twenty-nine when he made his Orioles debut on August 1, at Fenway Park against the Boston Red Sox.

"I signed with the Astros thinking I would get a chance to make the team out of Spring Training," Johnson said. "But they signed like seven major-league pitchers and figured I was seventeenth or eighteenth on the list and were not going anywhere with me. Then I end up in Triple-A Rochester with the Orioles. They also had guys like Pete Harnisch and Curt Schilling down at Triple-A, and I was not sure where I fit in.

"I knew the Orioles were really bad in 1988 and were contenders in 1989 but couldn't really put it into context at the time," Johnson said. "In 1988 I was in Buffalo, the Triple-A team of the Pirates, and concentrating on my job there. Then I was in Rochester for much of 1989 and was concentrating on the Redwings. News was much more sporadic back then. All we had was the newspapers and the highlights on TV.

"Back in 1988, I was just concerned with getting my fifteenth win to secure the team record for wins with Buffalo," Johnson continued. "I knew the Orioles were bad, but just did not realize how bad."

Johnson, whose son Steve would also pitch with the Orioles from 2012 to 2016, said that he kept getting word from the club not to pitch in Rochester because they were going to call him up. He ended up starting the second game of a double header in a 6–2 loss against the Red Sox. Although Johnson allowed five runs on eight hits in a losing effort, he gave the team 6 2/3 innings, allowing the bullpen to get a much-needed break.

The Orioles then had Johnson sit in the bullpen until August 8, when he started and threw a complete game, allowing one run on eight hits while striking out three and walking four in a 6–1 win over the Minnesota Twins at Memorial Stadium. Johnson followed that up with another complete-game performance on August 13, at home against the Red Sox. In that game, he allowed a run on six hits, struck out three, and walked two as the Orioles won 6–1. For his efforts, Johnson was named American League Player of the Week.

"I get called up in August and it was a strange time for me in the clubhouse. I was not with the team in Spring Training, so the manager didn't know me, the players did not really know me, and I did not know them," said Johnson. "I had my first start August 1 in the second game of a double header against the Boston Red Sox at Fenway Park. Even though I lost, I still pitched into the seventh inning. Then I sat around for a week before beating the Twins 6–1 and five days later I beat Boston 6–1 at Memorial Stadium. And just like that, *bam*, I'm American League Player of the Week."

Entering the 1989 season, Johnson said he never imagined pitching for his hometown team in the middle of a pennant race.

"I didn't think a team that lost 107 games the previous season would want to take a chance on a twenty-nine-year-old rookie like myself," Johnson said. "I figured they would be a team in rebuilding mode and I was not getting my hopes up as much as I wanted to play for my hometown team."

Johnson would pitch well in spurts for the Orioles down the stretch but would lose seven of his final eight decisions after the win over the Red Sox. Still, with role players stepping up, relying on a four-man rotation, key players like Tettleton and Cal Ripken Jr. contributing on offense, and a solid group of fielders on defense, the

Orioles—who trailed the Blue Jays by as much as 2 1/2 games on September 17—still had a chance to win the division in the final week of the season.

The season would end with a six-game road trip that included three in Milwaukee and three in Toronto. Baltimore took two of three from the Brewers, including a 4–0 win on September 27 in the series finale. In that game, Milacki allowed no runs on five hits with five walks in 6 1/3 innings. Tettleton gave the Orioles all the offense they would need when he hit a three-run homer off starter Jerry Reuss in the top of the fifth. Cal Ripken Jr. knocked in an insurance run with an RBI single in the top of the eighth off reliever Chuck Crim.

Heading into the three-game series against the Blue Jays in the SkyDome, the Orioles were one game back in the race for the AL East division crown. This was six years before the wild card was first used in the baseball playoff system, so the mission for both teams was obvious: win or go home. The Orioles had to win two of three to guarantee a one-game playoff or sweep and advance to the ALCS against the Oakland Athletics.

The pitching match-ups were set to be as follows (Orioles pitcher listed second): Todd Stottlemyre (7–7) vs. Jeff Ballard (18–8), Jimmy Key (13–14) vs. Pete Harnisch (5–9), and Jose Nunez (0–0) vs. Bob Milacki (14–12).

With so much on the line, the series took on a feeling of a de facto playoff series. The Orioles wanted nothing more than to cap the greatest turnaround in baseball history with a division title, and the Blue Jays wanted nothing more than to allow the clock to strike midnight on their Cinderella season (as well as winning the division). Phil Bradley did his part on the first pitch of the game when he hit a home run off Stottlemyre.

Ballard appeared determined to make that run stick, pitching seven shutout innings before allowing a leadoff single to left fielder

Mookie Wilson in the bottom of the eighth. Ballard then got Fred McGriff to hit into a fielder's choice before manager Frank Robinson replaced him with Olson.

This is when the inning fell apart. Tom Lawless, who was pinch running for McGriff, stole second base and advanced to third on a ground out by designated hitter George Bell. Olson then threw a wild pitch that got past backup catcher Jamie Quirk, which allowed Lawless to score and tie the game. Olson recovered to strike out third baseman Kelly Gruber, but the damage was already done. The Blue Jays would go on to win the game 2–1 after center fielder Lloyd Moseby hit a game-winning RBI single in the bottom of the 11th off Mark Williamson.

Now there was zero margin for error. The team's entire season and championship aspirations came down to winning the final two games of the series. This task became more difficult in the hours after losing the first game. The SkyDome, now known as Rogers Centre, opened in June 1989 and there was still construction debris in and around the stadium. Harnisch discovered this out first hand when he put his foot through a nail as he walked back to the hotel after the game.

The injury meant the Orioles would need a new starter for the second game of the series. Robinson opted to turn to Dave Johnson, who entered the series on anything but a roll. In his last appearance, Johnson had lasted just 4 2/3 innings, allowing four runs while striking out four and walking two in a 7–3 loss at the Brewers on September 26. By comparison, Harnisch allowed three runs on three hits and struck out five in 6 1/3 innings in a 5–3 win over the Brewers on September 25.

Johnson said those performances are what Robinson used to set his rotation for the Blue Jays series. He added that he found out he was getting the start in a unique manner.

"My original plan for that Saturday game in Toronto was to be out in the bullpen," Johnson said. "[Former Orioles bullpen coach] Elrod [Hendricks] had a tradition where he would put two balls into the shoes of whoever was the starting pitcher that night. When I got to the SkyDome, I saw the balls were in my shoes. At first, I thought it was a joke or Elrod made some sort of mistake. Then I found out about Pete Harnisch stepping on the nail and the ball is now in my hands in the biggest game of the year, and really the biggest game of my career at that point."

Johnson said the reality of the moment did not truly sink in until he stepped onto the pitcher's mound. A year before, he was traveling in a bus for Triple-A Buffalo in the Pirates organization. Now, he was playing in front of fifty thousand fans in a nationally televised game trying to lead his hometown team into the playoffs.

At the time, Johnson said he did not even think about what the turnaround from the previous season meant to the players who were on the previous year's team or the fans who supported them through such a trying season.

"Remember, this was a time before cell phones, social media, and the Internet," Johnson said. "The only way we got scores back then was in the newspaper box scores, the evening sportscast, and maybe *SportsCenter* if the hotel had cable. I was aware of the Orioles' losing streak but did not really pay to close attention to it because, even though I'm from Baltimore, I had my own concerns trying to make the team in Pittsburgh.

"Also, I wasn't with the Orioles at all in 1988 and was acquired late in spring training in 1989, so I had no connection to that streak. But I did understand just how important that game at Toronto was to the season and to my career. I was not going to shy away from the challenge."

Unlike the first game of the series, the Blue Jays struck first as Bell's RBI single to right field drove in Moseby—who led off the game with a walk—to give Toronto a 1–0 lead. Johnson said he got down on himself as he got to the dugout before Robinson reamed him out and reminded him there were still eight innings to go and the team was capable of its own comeback.

Johnson settled down after his shaky start, allowing just two runs on two hits with three walks over seven innings in a gritty, workman-like performance. True to Robinson's word, the Orioles responded in the top of the third when, with two outs, Cal Ripken Jr. and Randy Milligan connected on a run-scoring double and single, respectively, off starter Jimmy Key to give the Orioles a 2–1 lead. Bradley's two-out RBI single off Key in the fourth extended the lead to 3–1.

The Orioles and Johnson maintained control of the game until the bottom of the eighth, when he gave up a leadoff walk to second baseman Nelson Liriano. Johnson was done for the day and replaced by Kevin Hickey, who then walked pinch hitter Manuel Lee (which would be the only batter he'd face). With runners on first and second and no outs, Robinson now turned to veteran Mark Williamson to get out of the jam. After Moseby's sacrifice bunt moved the runners to second and third, Wilson hit an RBI single to left, McGriff hit an RBI single to right, and Bell hit a sacrifice fly—all off Williamson—as the Blue Jays took a 4–3 lead.

Baltimore had one more chance to rally back again in the top of the ninth. However, the team's improbable season would fall one comeback short. The Blue Jays brought in closer Tom Henke, who struck out Tettleton, got Orsulak to ground out, and struck out Larry Sheets to end the game. Along with the loss came the end to the team's hopes for an improbable division title.

While Baltimore rebounded to win the regular-season finale,

7–5, it was too little too late. The "Why Not?" season became the not now season for the Orioles, who finished the 1989 campaign with an 87–75 record, good enough for second place in the AL East.

Ripken Jr. said being involved in a pennant race again was something he appreciated more at that point in his career. After experiencing so much success in his first two seasons, Ripken admitted he expected to be playing meaningful October baseball much more than he did.

"We changed out a lot of players after 1988, but there were no expectations for us in 1989," Ripken Jr. said. "Then we beat the Boston Red Sox on Opening Day, got on a roll, and put together a special season right until that final weekend in Toronto.

"When you go through something like we did in 1988, you learn to appreciate winning that much more," Ripken Jr. continued. "It felt good to win. Doing something to help affect the outcome of the game—whether it was turning a big double play, moving a runner over with a sacrifice, or coming through with a clutch hit—they all have more meaning when you're in a pennant race."

The 34-game turnaround revitalized the fanbase, helped bring credibility back to the franchise planning to move into a new ballpark in three years, and went a long way toward making the team and city forget the pain from just a year before. There was also plenty of recognition for the turnaround. Robinson was named the AL Manager of the Year and Olson became the first reliever to win the AL Rookie of the Year Award. Olson also set an AL rookie record with 27 saves and finished with a record of 5–2 and a 1.69 ERA to go along with 90 strikeouts in 85 innings pitched.

Olson said the success of the 1989 Orioles was not due to any one player, but the sum of the parts of a team that came together with a variety of individuals stepping up and contributing when others were struggling or injured.

"That 1989 Orioles team was one where every player played an important role at some point during the season," Olson said. "It could have been all year like Jeff Ballard or Mickey Tettleton, or just a few weeks like when Dave Johnson gave us a boost in August moving forward. It's the type of team I haven't seen come together since. We just did not know any better at the time."

Olson said having just a handful of players on the team who experienced the losing streak from the year before allowed the Orioles to move forward quicker than they might have otherwise.

"For me, the only ones that had a bad taste about the team from the year before were the fans," Olson said. "Every Opening Day is like a brand-new beginning. It was the chance to start over and forget about what happened the year before."

Johnson said coming up short in Toronto still stings, but he will always remember how the fans rallied behind the club during that year, even when they returned to Baltimore after that season-ending series in Toronto.

"While we came up just short, it was a heck of a ride and it was great to be part of a season that many fans even today tell me was their favorite as an Orioles fan," Johnson said. "We had a confluence of things come together well in 1989, just like the team had a confluence of things go wrong in 1988. Baseball is a unique sport like that in that it does not take much for a team to get on a roll or for a team to hit a long losing streak. Winning and losing are contagious in sports at all levels."

Richie Bancells said that, despite how the season ended, 1989 will always be one he will look fondly upon—especially given the historic struggles the team faced the year before.

"Going through what we went through in 1988 made 1989 that much more special," Bancells said. "We weren't supposed to be a contender, and because it came out of nowhere the fans were that much more behind the team. Something special happened that season, something that does not come around all too often.

"We were so close to winning the division," Bancells recalls. "It was upsetting that we couldn't bring it home for the fans that weekend in Toronto, but that did not take away from the magical ride that season was."

"I still hear from Oriole fans that the 1989 'Why Not?' team was their favorite Orioles team of all times," Orsulak said. "I truly believe we were a big bat away from winning the division. Had we gotten past Toronto, I loved our chances against the Oakland A's because we were the only American League team to have a winning record against them, and they went on to win the World Series.

"Back then, only two teams in each league qualified for the play-offs, so to be playing meaningful baseball right down to the last series was special," Orsulak continued. "You have to appreciate the moment when it happens because you don't know if it will ever come again."

Devereaux called the season a great run for the organization, and he was so impressed with how the fans came out to back the team after they returned from Toronto.

"We were right there until the end and it was just heartbreaking to come up short," Devereaux said. "It was a hard way to end the season as we fought right until the end. Then for the fans to hold a parade and celebration for us even though we did not win was unbelievable. That is a season I know I will never forget."

Michael Gibbons said as slow and flawed as the 1988 Orioles were, the 1989 Orioles were just as fun, enthusiastic, and naïve enough to not concern themselves with the near-historic run they almost completed.

"That 'Why Not?' Orioles team was fun to watch, and they were simply a good ballclub, with great characters like Mickey Tettleton and Jeff Ballard and Gregg Olson and of course Cal Ripken Jr. was still at the top of his game," Gibbons said. "The fans were so excited about them and wanted nothing more than to beat the Blue Jays that season.

"That season-ending series at the Blue Jays was so nerve-racking and the ending was so disappointing. When Phil Bradley hit that home run to lead off the first game of the series in the SkyDome, I literally fell out of my seat in front of my TV set. While it did not work out in the end, it was still an amazing year to be an Orioles fan and helped take the sting out of that losing streak from just a year prior."

Mills said there is a direct correlation between the Orioles' success that season, recognizing the missteps of recent years, and returning to the core values that the team established during their championship runs.

"The success of 1989 was a direct result of getting away from the mistakes of years past," Mills said. "They traded away some of the older players and let others go and brought in a core that not only helped in 1989 but were integral parts of the teams in 1992 and 1993, which were very competitive and fun to watch. There was also the trade that brought in Brady Anderson and the acquisition of players like Mike Devereaux and Phil Bradley who really helped people forget about 1988."

Garceau agreed. He said he enjoyed everything about watching and covering the Orioles in 1989. He added that fans could relate to the players on the roster and wanted nothing more than to see them knock off the Blue Jays, who would go on to lose in the ALCS to the eventual World Series–champion Athletics.

"This was a team in 1989 that did not really heat up until late May," Garceau said. "Then they get a nice run and by July had a 7 1/2-game lead. They just battled all the way to the last week of the season when they came up just short against the Blue Jays.

"It was such a fun team with guys like Phil Bradley and Brady

Anderson and Joe Orsulak playing hard and scrapping for each win," Garceau continued. "After such a miserable season in 1988, it was great to see the team come back in 1989. I have never had more fun covering a team than I did with the Orioles that season."

Ken Rosenthal called the Orioles' 1989 season one of the most enjoyable he has ever covered. "With everything that took place in 1988, the run the Orioles had in 1989 was so special," Rosenthal said. "I never had more fun covering a team than I did with the Orioles that season.

With a manager that was a Hall of Fame player, a roster of up-and-comers, a future hall of famer in Cal Ripken Jr. and a solid bullpen, the Orioles appeared poised to turn the corner in their effort to restore long-term respectability back into the franchise. However, as quickly as the turnaround came, it would not be sustained.

Chapter Twelve

POSTSCRIPT

Any momentum the Orioles may have had heading into 1990 was gone before the season began. The start was delayed due to a lockout; a labor dispute which kept some players busy dealing with negotiations while many others were not able to properly prepare and train for the upcoming season.

For the Orioles, this began with starting pitcher Jeff Ballard. The ace of the staff who had led the team in wins the previous two seasons and was sixth in the Cy Young Award voting in 1989, Ballard underwent two surgeries to remove bone spurs from his left shoulder prior to the season. He was also the team's player representative with the union, which required that he attend drawn-out bargaining sessions in New York as the lockout unfolded and the season was in jeopardy.

Ballard said the surgeries, combined with the labor negotiations, played a factor in the struggles he faced the rest of his career. He posted just a 2–11 record in 1990 and was 8–23 for the Orioles over his final two seasons. Ballard would eventually make it back to the majors with Pittsburgh in 1993, but his career came to a screeching halt after he broke his neck in a serious automobile accident in Idaho in January 1995.

"Between [the surgeries], the lockout, and the negotiations, my rehab did not go as it should have and I was just awful in 1990. I was even worse by 1991 because my mechanics were all messed up after the surgery. It took me years to get those mechanics back, which happened right before the accident that ended my career."

Despite Ballard's regression, pitching did not appear to be the biggest issue for the Orioles in 1990. Pete Harnisch continued to develop and won 11 games with a team-high 122 strikeouts, while Dave Johnson led the team with 13 wins. In addition, the bullpen continued to thrive as closer Gregg Olson made the All-Star team and recorded 37 saves while Mark Williamson won eight games with a 2.21 ERA as the team's other top reliever.

But the 1990 season would also represent one the organization and fanbase were hoping would be the arrival of the next great pitching star. That pitcher, Ben McDonald, came to the Orioles as a direct result of their poor performance in 1988, meaning they would get the first overall pick in the 1989 MLB June Amateur Draft. They used that pick to select McDonald out of Louisiana State University.

To many, McDonald had the highest grade by scouts at that point for a player coming out of college. He was deemed a can't-miss prospect by just about every player development department, and it appeared to be a no-brainer for the Orioles to select him as the centerpiece of their rebuilding efforts.

In McDonald's junior season at LSU, he was named an All-American while posting a record of 14–4 with a 3.49 ERA and a Southeastern Conference record 202 strikeouts.

McDonald signed with the Orioles on August 19, 1989, and made his major-league debut on September 6—just 18 days later. He would eventually join the starting rotation by midseason of 1990 and would win his first five decisions, which included a complete-game shutout on July 21, 1990, against the Chicago White Sox.

In that game, which the Orioles won 2–0, McDonald allowed no runs on four hits while striking out five and walking one. Coincidentally, the losing pitcher in that game was Jack McDowell, the losing pitcher for Chicago when the Orioles broke their 21-game losing streak in 1988. McDonald finished his rookie season with an 8–5 record, a 2.43 ERA, and 65 strikeouts in 118 2/3 innings.

The Orioles had high hopes for McDonald moving forward, but while he went on to have a serviceable major-league career, he never lived up to the expectations associated with being the top overall pick. McDonald would go 58–53 for the Orioles between 1989 and 1995, which included winning at least thirteen games from 1993 to 1995.

McDonald would go on to sign with the Milwaukee Brewers as a free agent in 1996, where he pitched his final two seasons before shoulder injuries forced him to retire at the age of twenty-nine. He ended his career with a record of 78–70. McDonald would eventually reunite with the Orioles, with whom he now serves as an occasional member of the team's game broadcasts.

"Big Ben had all the tools to be an ace No. 1 starter at the major-league level," Keith Mills said. "He showed flashes of it with the Orioles, but injuries really derailed his career. His arm and shoulder had so many miles on it by the time he was drafted that it was just a matter of time before that caught up to him. That's why draft picks were and remain such a crapshoot in baseball compared to some of the other sports. No one questioned the rationale for the Orioles taking Ben McDonald in that draft, it was just the case of it not panning out as they expected it would for them and Ben for that matter."

* * *

Getting back to the 1990 season, the team's larger issues that year were on offense. Catcher Mickey Tettleton went from hitting 26 home runs and a .258 batting average in 1989 to just 15 and .223 in 1990. Third baseman Craig Worthington went from 15 home runs and 70 RBIs to eight home runs and 44 RBIs. Cal Ripken Jr. did hit a team-high 21 home runs and led the team with 84 RBIs, but his batting average dipped to .250, one of the lowest of his career. Second baseman Billy Ripken actually led the team in batting average that year, when he hit a career-best .301.

The combination of Ballard's struggles and the offense's regression led the team to a fifth-place finish in the AL East with a 76–84 record. Ripken Jr. said they were lulled into a false sense of security after the great year in 1989. In hindsight, Ripken believes the Orioles should have stayed the course and continued to build around their young core.

Instead of returning to their original formula for success, the organization made a drastic move and traded outfielder Steve Finley and pitchers Curt Schilling and Pete Harnisch to the Houston Astros in an ill-advised deal for Glenn Davis prior to the 1991 season.

That season, the final one at Memorial Stadium, was even worse as the team posted a 67–95 record and finished dead last in the AL East. The team also replaced manager Frank Robinson with first base coach Johnny Oates after the team started 13–24. Robinson ended his managerial tenure with the club with a record of 230–285 over parts of four seasons.

"We had a chance to continue to build for the future," Cal Ripken Jr. said. "There was a core of talent in place, but the belief was we were just a big bat away from really contending. So, they traded for Glenn Davis, which for a variety of reasons did not work out, and the players we traded away all went on to have long, successful careers elsewhere."

Cal Ripken Jr. and others who played with him on the 1988 team said they try to use that season as a teachable moment both in their lives and working with young players. That team will always be associated with the 21-game losing streak. At the same time, that team's legacy goes much deeper.

For fans, the joy they felt in 1989 would not have been possible without the pain they suffered in 1988. For the Orioles, the moves they made as a response to the 1988 season provided several core players, including outfielders Brady Anderson and Mike Devereaux, catcher Chris Hoiles, and closer Gregg Olson, who helped the team as they transitioned from Memorial Stadium to Oriole Park at Camden Yards.

While Devereaux did not play on the 1988 team, he can relate to just how fleeting success can be in baseball. He said the 1990 and 1991 campaigns were difficult to handle after experiencing so much success on the field as a rookie.

"Baseball is a sport with such highs and lows from one year to the next," Devereaux said. "It is how you handle them that is important. Those years in 1990 and 1991 were such bad years and it made me appreciate what we had in 1989 even more. In 1989 we would have people offering to pay for our dinner and then in 1990 and 1991 we would be stopping to fill up for gas and fans would ask us 'Why is everything going wrong?'"

For Joe Orsulak, the 1988 season was an experience that helped keep everything in perspective for him both on and off the field.

"The lesson is when you have a chance to win, you need to take advantage of it because next year you could get injured or have a bad season," Orsulak said. "That opportunity may never come again. The 'Why Not?' year was really the only time I was in a true pennant race in my career."

Gregg Olson can attest to just how fleeting success can be in professional sports in general and baseball specifically. After arriving as the savior of the bullpen in 1988, he developed into one of the sport's best closers through the 1993 season.

In August 1993, Olson suffered a torn elbow ligament that put him on the shelf for the remainder of the year. That season, he finished with 29 saves and a career-low 1.60 ERA, but the Orioles had severe concerns about the injury and Olson's future. Instead, they opted to sign veteran closer Lee Smith, who played the previous year with the New York Yankees, to anchor their bullpen in 1994.

In the following years, Olson appeared with the Atlanta Braves (1994), Cleveland Indians (1995), Kansas City Royals (1995 and 1997), Detroit Tigers (1996), Houston Astros (1996), and Minnesota Twins (1997). Olson was not sure if he would ever experience success again, similar to what he had in Baltimore.

That changed in 1998 when he came back to save 30 games as the closer for the expansion Arizona Diamondbacks. He would remain with the team in 1999, when they won 100 games and captured the NL West title in just their second year of existence. Olson pitched the following two seasons for the Los Angeles Dodgers before retiring after the 2001 season, finishing his career with 217 saves, a 40–39 record, 588 strikeouts, and a 3.46 ERA in 672 innings pitched. He was inducted into the Orioles Hall of Fame in 2008.

"It was just exciting to be in the playoff race in 1989 with the Orioles," Olson said. "That is not something I got to experience all too often in my career, and it made for a great season.

"I loved that [1999] Diamondbacks team because it was a no-nonsense group that came together and took care of business without any clubhouse drama," Olson said.

Olson said that same attitude the Diamondbacks showed in 1999 was similar to the Orioles ten years earlier. He believes that was something he noticed was missing on the team in 1988.

"I'm not sure the team chemistry was there in 1988 with the

Orioles," Olson said. "We just had a great group of guys who loved to play baseball during that 'Why Not?' season in 1989. In a day and age where Sabermetrics is examined so closely, I think chemistry in the clubhouse is something that can be easily forgotten about. That chemistry went a long way to helping us get through that 1989 season."

Olson said the turnaround between 1988 and 1989 is what makes sports so enjoyable to play, watch, and support from both a fan and athlete's perspective.

"Every year is a fresh start in baseball," Olson said. "You need to make sure you enjoy the moment each season, because you never know what the next season will bring. I can attest to that."

Michael Gibbons agrees. "When you look at the 1988 roster, it was not a world beater of a lineup or pitching staff, but there was definitely some talent on that team," Gibbons said. "But that was a season where the baseball gods were against them and anything that could go wrong absolutely did. Then in 1989, the team filled with youth and enthusiasm came within an eyelash of turning in one of the most remarkable worst to first finishes ever in sports."

* * *

The Orioles would go on to be playoff contenders for much of the 1990s. This included in 1992 through 1994, when they remained in the hunt for the AL East title. They ended up in third place in 1992 and 1993, seven and ten games back, respectively, of the Toronto Blue Jays, who won back-to-back World Series titles those years. In 1994, the club was in second place in the AL East and in contention for the Wild Card before the players' strike cancelled the rest of the season and playoffs.

Devereaux was among those players who helped keep the team

competitive in the early years at Camden Yards. His breakout season came in 1992—the first year at the new ballpark—when the center fielder batted .276 with 24 home runs and 107 RBIs in 156 games.

Just as impressive during that time was Devereaux's defense, as he and Brady Anderson came up with one highlight catch after another. The team would eventually advance to the ALCS in 1996 (a feat they would repeat the following year without Devereaux when they led the AL East wire-to-wire).

As for Devereaux, his greatest postseason success came in 1995 when he won the NLCS Most Valuable Player Award as a member of the Atlanta Braves. In that series against the Cincinnati Reds, Devereaux drove in the game-winning RBI in the 10th of Game One and hit a three-run home run in Game Four. The Braves went on to defeat the Cleveland Indians in the World Series.

Devereaux, who also played for the White Sox and Rangers, retired in 1998 with a career .254 average, 105 home runs, and 480 RBIs. After retiring, he would transition to coaching, which would include stints with two of the Orioles' minor league affiliates: the low-Single-A Delmarva Shorebirds and the Single-A Frederick Keys. He entered 2018 as the hitting coach for the Reds' Double-A affiliate, the Pensacola Blue Wahoos of the Southern League.

"It was a real competition with us back in the day between me and Brady," said Devereaux who, along with Anderson, were dubbed "Batman and Robin" during the 1992 season. "We were overachievers for most of my career, with the exception of the 1996 team that advanced to the ALCS.

"That's why you play the games and why every one counts," Devereaux continued. "I hate when I hear people say those one-run losses in April don't matter because you have so many games to play. But those games at the beginning of the season count just as much as those in September and October. It is tough to get to a World Series and even tougher to win one. I was extremely lucky to experience all I did in my career and now I enjoy sharing those experiences with the young players of today as a coach."

* * *

After the success of the 1996 and 1997 seasons, years of risky free agent signings, poor drafting and player development, and instability in the front office and at manager combined to ensure the Orioles would post fourteen consecutive losing seasons.

It was not until the club began rebuilding around 2008, along with the arrival of manager Buck Showalter in 2010, that the team would return to some semblance of the Oriole Way. They would make the playoffs in 2012, 2014, and 2016, which included a trip to the ALDS in 2012, the ALCS in 2014, and an AL Wild Card in 2016. However, despite being the winningest team in the American League from 2012 to 2016, the Orioles once again fell apart in the last month of the 2017 season, which led to a last-place finish in the AL East. This carried over to the team's most recent last-place finish in 2018, when they had the worst record in baseball. The club then decided to move on from general manager Dan Duquette and Showalter, and entered 2019 trying to rebuild once again under new GM Mike Elias and skipper Brandon Hyde.

"When you look at the larger picture of Orioles history, especially from the mid-1960s through 1997, the team still had one of the best records in baseball over that time—even when you take the 1986, 1987, and even 1988 seasons into the equation," Gibbons said. "The Orioles were that good for that long. Unfortunately, the team then had that stretch of fourteen-straight losing seasons beginning in 1998 before turning things around in 2012."

Fred Lynn said the 1988 team is one he will always be associated with. Even thirty years later, he is still dumbfounded how they lost that many games in a row; a streak he would never wish on any other player.

"What are the odds that a Major League Baseball team loses that many games in a row?" Lynn asks. "Think about it: if you flip a coin twenty-two times, there is almost no chance that it lands on the same side twenty-one times in a row."

At the same time, Lynn points out one of the great aspects of sports is how quickly even the worst teams can turn their fortunes around with the right moves and just a bit of luck.

"To see what the Orioles did in 1989 shows you how just a few moves and breaks can change the course of a season and a franchise," Lynn said. "It doesn't take much to turn things around if done right. If it's not done right, then a team can be set back even further."

For many of those on that infamous team, their experience turned into a life lesson that they try to share with younger generations. John Habyan said that while he divided his time between the major league club and Triple-A Rochester that season, it was hard for anyone associated with the club not to be affected by the losing streak.

"There were plenty of guys that were on the main roster the whole season and had a much different perspective than me," Habyan said. "That whole season was such a haze. I know I was there for some of it and in Rochester for other parts of it. It was just a rough season altogether."

Habyan added that the losing streak made him a stronger player who understood the true difference between the thrill of victory and the agony of defeat.

"A season like that will toughen a player up if they can get through it," Habyan said. "I played eight more seasons in the majors after that and had a pretty good career, which I appreciated that much more after going through that 1988 season."

Habyan said his memories from that season also offer great lessons he can instill in his players in his current role as pitching coach at Hofstra University in New York.

"I use that season as a great learning tool," Habyan said. "When my players deal with a losing streak or begin to struggle, I let them know I've felt their pain . . . *literally.*

"I have them Google the 1988 Orioles and *Sports Illustrated,*" Habyan continued. "Then, they see the cover with Billy Ripken and that frustrated look on his face and I point out that I was a part of that team. That puts a lot of things into perspective for them."

Jose Bautista takes a different approach when working with potential future major-league pitchers as a coach with the Birmingham Barons, the Double-A affiliate of the Chicago White Sox.

"I don't dwell on that 1988 season too much or bring it up with the young pitchers I am coaching," Bautista said. "I know after what I went through that there are going to be struggles at various points in the season. I try to just stress the positives. I won't even show the pitchers video of poor performances."

Harold Baines has a unique perspective of the losing streak. Along with recording the final out for the Chicago White Sox in the game the Orioles finally won on April 29, 1988, he is considered among the most popular players in both teams' history. Baines experienced the highs and lows of both franchises. Even so, he was inducted into the Orioles Hall of Fame in 2009. This came a year after the White Sox unveiled a bronze statue of him at U.S. Cellular Field. He was the seventh person to be recognized with such an honor on the outfield concourse.

"As a player, I always tried to work hard and do the best that I could," said Baines, who as of 2018 still worked with the White Sox as a team ambassador. "I am just lucky that I played in two cities that really appreciated how I played and my approach to the game."

Baines said he remembers talking with Cal Ripken Jr. about the losing streak when they were teammates in Baltimore in the 1990s. Baines admits he believes losing 21 games in a row is harder to do than winning 21 games straight.

"I remember Cal telling me that they just tried to go out there every day with hopes to win a game and finally end that streak," Baines said. "Unfortunately for them, each game they found another way to lose. That must have been unbelievably tough to go through."

Baines said he never experienced a losing streak quite like that 1988 season, but dealt with many struggles throughout his career. He knows how difficult those times were for him and cannot even imagine what it had to be like to be on the team that year.

"I am sure players were trying everything they could think of to turn things around," Baines said. "It could have been anything from changing their shoes, trying a different glove or bat, altering their batting stance, or anything that might have made a difference during that time."

Roy Firestone said no sports dynasty lasts forever, and the Orioles were no exception. He added that there is a fine line from a team having to just retool compared to rebuilding, and the decisions a team makes regarding such an approach can set the stage for how a team performs for decades to come.

The NFL's New England Patriots, who won five Super Bowls and appeared in three others over a seventeen-year span, remained relevant by knowing how to draft smartly (quarterback Tom Brady was a sixth-round draft pick in 2000) and would rather cut ties with a player a year too early than a year too late.

By comparison, the NBA's Boston Celtics won sixteen world titles between 1957 and 1986. However, draft disasters—like losing 1986 top draft pick Len Bias out of the University of Maryland to a drug overdose the day after his selection, along with holding on to aging veterans like Kevin McHale and Robert Parish long past their prime—took the team decades to recover from. The Celtics did not win their seventeenth title until Kevin Garnett, Paul Pierce, and Ray Allen helped them raise another championship banner in 2008.

"Through the 1960s and into the 1970s, the Orioles could do no wrong," Firestone said. "But the 1980s and into the 1990s, the team, with few exceptions, could do no right when it came to personnel decisions."

Firestone highlighted two trades that point out the differences between the Orioles prior to 1983 and after that World Series championship team.

"A perfect example was the ten-player trade with the Yankees in 1976 that brought in McGregor and Dempsey, among others," Firestone said. "Then, by 1991, the Orioles traded for Glenn Davis with the belief that they acquired the big batter they thought they needed.

"Instead, Davis suffered a freakish nerve injury in his neck and was never the same player again," Firestone said. Meanwhile Pete Harnish, Steve Finley, and Curt Schilling went on to have long careers. "At the end of the day, it came down to personnel on the field and in the front office. The team had the talent and then they lost it."

After retiring in 2001, Ripken Jr. remained active in baseball through various professional and charitable ventures. This included joining with his brother Billy to form Ripken Baseball, which owns and operates youth baseball complexes in Aberdeen, Maryland; Myrtle Beach, South Carolina; and Pigeon Forge, Tennessee. The Ripkens also own the Aberdeen IronBirds, a short-season Single-A affiliate of the Orioles. At one point, Ripken Baseball also hosted the Cal Ripken World Series, which brought youth baseball teams from all over the world for an annual tournament in Maryland.

In addition, Cal and Billy also formed the Cal Ripken Sr. Foundation, the mission of which is to build character and teach critical life lessons to at-risk youth living in America's most distressed communities. Among the initiatives spearheaded by the foundation is the Cal Ripken Sr. Foundation Youth Development Parks program. According to the foundation, these multipurpose, synthetic turf, low-maintenance facilities are designed to provide a cohesive recreational and educational experience for children, particularly in at-risk communities. Included in these parks is one built on the site where Memorial Stadium once stood on 33rd Street in Baltimore.

Ripken Jr. said all these initiatives are designed in part to continue the lessons and legacy established by his father, both with the Orioles and in the community. Ripken Jr. added that looking back now, he can view the 21-game losing streak in 1988 as an educational experience, something he admits he did not think would be the case at the time.

"The losing streak was a miserable thing to go through, but you learn to appreciate winning more because of it," Ripken Jr. said.

Ripken Jr. said once the streak ended, he pushed himself to find different ways to keep himself and other players motivated, even as they spent the entire season in last place.

"At that point, you just have to find different ways to compete as a player," Ripken said on the end of the losing streak. "You just had to set goals for yourself for the week or the month or the second half of the season to help make the rest of the games meaningful. I remember trying to help other players in the team set similar individual goals for themselves to keep them focused and motivated."

Ripken said after winning the World Series in 1983, he figured like Brooks Robinson, Frank Robinson, Jim Palmer, and Earl Weaver, he would experience similar championships many more times before he retired. This was not the case.

"I would not wish a losing streak like that on anybody, but now I can look back and appreciate the wins even more than before," Ripken said. "Unless you go through something like this, you don't really know how to come back from it. It really is an individual lesson for people dealing with adversity."

Ripken said despite playing on as many losing teams as winning ones over his career, he knows getting a World Series ring and appearing in the playoffs two other times is way more than most players get to experience. As much as the 1988 season was difficult to endure and even look back on, he tries to look at the complete history of the Orioles during that era.

"It's all about perspective," Ripken Jr. said. "Think about the careers of players like Chipper Jones with the Atlanta Braves and Derek Jeter with the New York Yankees. Those are two players that were at least in the playoffs and competed for the World Series just about every year. Chipper Jones joined the Braves as they were in the midst of winning fourteen-straight divisional titles, winning a World Series, and playing in several others. Derek Jeter joins the Yankees just as they launched into their most recent dynasty, where he won five World Series titles and played in two others.

"For teams like the Braves and Yankees and players like Chipper and Derek, getting eliminated in the first round of the playoffs was considered a bad season. I would have loved to have had that feeling in my career. That is why you have to enjoy the run while it is going on because it may be the only chance you get."

Chapter 13

BREAKING DOWN THE
LOSING STREAK

April 4 (0–1): If one game could set the tone for an entire season, this was it. A franchise-record 55,392 fans turned out to watch the Orioles lose 12–0 to the Milwaukee Brewers on Opening Day at old Memorial Stadium in Baltimore.

The Brewers did most of their damage in the eighth, when they scored six times and sent eleven men to the plate. This included short-stop Dale Sveum, who hit a two-run home run off rookie reliever Oswald Peraza. Peraza allowed three earned runs and three hits while walking two in 1 2/3 innings in his major-league debut.

Mike Boddicker took the loss for the Orioles, as he allowed four runs on nine hits in 5 1/3 innings.

The loss tied a record for the most lopsided shutout defeat on Opening Day in American League history.

April 6 (0–2): The Orioles received much better pitching in their first night game of the season, but their anemic offense continued to sputter in a 3–1 loss to the Brewers.

Starting pitcher Mike Morgan turned in a solid performance as he threw a complete game, allowing three runs, six hits, and a walk while striking out two. However, Brewers starter Chris Bosio was even better as he scattered five hits and struck out two in a complete-game victory.

The Orioles led for much of this game after Eddie Murray reached on a single and later scored on a grounder by Larry Sheets in the bottom of the second. The Brewers responded by scoring all three of their runs with two outs in the top of the sixth. Brewers shortstop Dale Sveum tied the game at one with a home run while catcher B.J. Surhoff, who would later go on to be one of the most popular Orioles in team history in the late 1990s, drove in the remaining runs with a two-run double.

April 8 (0–3): In a lineup that included two first-ballot Hall of Famers, the Orioles' inability to score runs continued as they lost 3–0 to the host Cleveland Indians.

Indians starter Scott Bailes tossed a complete-game shutout as he allowed just three hits, struck out four, and walked three in a 113-pitch performance. The loss represented the first time the Orioles had dropped their first three games to start a season since 1984, the year after their last World Series victory.

Much like the previous game, the Orioles received a solid starting pitching performance. But again, one bad inning was all it took to cost them the game. Starter Mark Thurmond took the loss after allowing three runs on six hits while striking out three and walking two in 6 2/3 innings.

Thurmond got two outs in the bottom of the seventh before allowing a single and two walks to load the bases. Reliever Doug Sisk then walked Indians catcher Andy Allanson to force in the first run.

Second baseman Julio Franco drove in the Indians' final two runs on an infield single.

April 9 (0–4): Neither the pitching, hitting, nor defense fared well in this game for the Orioles as the Indians cruised to a 12–1 victory.

The Indians pounded out twenty hits off five different Oriole pitchers. Every starter had at least one hit, including right fielder Cory Snyder, who went 3-for-5 with a double, home run, and three runs batted in. First baseman Willie Upshaw went 3-for-4 at the plate with a home run and two RBIs of his own. Cleveland starter and knuckleballer Tom Candiotti went the distance, allowing just one run on eight hits while striking out six and walking three to pick up the victory.

Most of the Indians' offense came in the second and third, when they scored five and four runs, respectively. Mike Boddicker's struggles continued as he allowed five earned runs and eight hits in just 1 2/3 innings. Reliever Mark Williamson did not fare any better as he allowed four earned runs on four hits while walking two and striking out one in just 2/3 of an inning.

Designated hitter Larry Sheets's RBI single in the top of the ninth was the only bright spot in a horribly played game by Baltimore. In the loss, the Orioles committed three errors, which included outfielder Joe Orsulak dropping a fly ball and Williamson throwing the ball away on a pickoff attempt.

April 10 (0–5): One of the many frustrations during the losing streak was the team's ability to make ordinary players look extraordinary. That was the case in this game as they dropped their fifth straight by a score of 6–3 to the Indians.

Indians starter Rich Yett, who posted a career 22–24 record

with a 4.95 ERA in six major-leagues seasons with the Indians and Minnesota Twins, allowed three runs on seven hits while striking out two and walking two over 6 1/3 innings to pick up the win. Shortstop Jay Bell and outfielder Carmelo Castillo drove in two runs each for the Indians, who broke the game open with four runs in the bottom of the fourth—all off veteran starter Scott McGregor.

McGregor allowed five runs (four earned) on seven hits while striking out two and walking one in 3 2/3 innings in a losing effort. In a sign of just how bad the Orioles had played to start the season, Baltimore recorded its most prolific offensive output to date. Second baseman Billy Ripken had two hits and drove in three runs while Orsulak had three hits. The loss matched their second-worst start in team history, tying the 0–5 set by the team to begin the 1978 season.

April 11 (0–6): Sloppy play, shaky starting pitching, and poor hitting all contributed to the Orioles' 7–2 loss to the Indians. The 0–6 record tied the 1955 Orioles for the worst start in franchise history.

Facing a lineup with five left-handed batters, Indians southpaw Greg Swindell pitched a complete game, allowing two earned runs on eight hits while striking out eight and walking none. Offensively, designated hitter Pat Tabler and right fielder Cory Snyder drove in two runs each for the Indians, who broke open a 2–2 tie with two runs in the sixth and another three in the seventh.

Starter Mike Morgan allowed seven earned runs on eight hits while striking out two and walking four in 6 2/3 innings. Rick Schu drove in Baltimore's lone runs of the game with a two-run home run in the top of the fifth. The hit represented the Orioles' first home run of the season, the last team in the majors to hit one out.

Not long after the game, the team fired manager Cal Ripken Sr. and replaced him with Hall of Fame outfielder and former Oriole Frank Robinson. Robinson, the first African American manager in team history, had been working as a special assistant to owner Edward Bennett Williams.

April 12 (0–7): There was a new manager, a new lineup, and a new opponent, but the result was the same as the Orioles set a new record for the worse start in franchise history with a 6–1 loss to the visiting Kansas City Royals.

An announced crowd of just 11,180 came out to witness Robinson's managerial debut. Royals pitchers Mark Gubicza and Dan Quisenberry combined to hold the Orioles to a single unearned run. Gubicza picked up the win after allowing the unearned run on two hits while striking out six and walking five over seven innings.

Trailing 1–0, the Royals got all the offense they needed when they scored three times in the top of the fourth thanks to back-to-back home runs by second baseman Frank White (a two-run shot) and outfielder Bo Jackson off starter Oswaldo Peraza. A right-hander making his first major-league start, Peraza allowed five earned runs on five hits while striking out two and walking four in just four innings.

Joe Orsulak led off the game with a single and scored the team's lone run in the bottom of the first on a sacrifice fly by Cal Ripken Jr. The RBI was Ripken's first of the season.

April 13 (0–8): Even replacing three left-handed starters with right-handed bats could not stop the Orioles' freefall, who lost 9–3 to the Royals.

Frank Robinson inserted right fielder Tito Landrum, left fielder Wade Rowdon, and catcher Carl Nichols (to replace Fred Lynn, Jeff Stone, and Terry Kennedy), hoping for a spark against left-hander Floyd Bannister. Instead, Bannister allowed two runs (one earned) on two hits while striking out five and walking four en route to picking up his second win of the season.

The Royals broke the game open with two runs in the third and three more in the fourth. Right fielder Danny Tartabull went 4-for-5 and drove in four runs, while third baseman Kevin Seitzer (two RBIs) and shortstop Kurt Stillwell had three hits apiece for the Royals in an 18-hit barrage.

Most of the Royals damage was off starter Mark Thurmond, who allowed six earned runs on ten hits while striking out two and walking two in just 3 2/3 innings. The loss dropped him to 0–2 on the season.

Nichols, Landrum, and Rowdon went a combined 1-for-9 with a walk and a strikeout in the loss. Rick Schu, Cal Ripken Jr., and Eddie Murray drove in the runs for the Orioles, with the latter's coming off his first home run of the season. The game represented the one thousandth of Ripken's career and the 935th game he played consecutively.

April 14 (0–9): During the streak, the Orioles appeared to invent new ways to lose games. This game was no exception, as they committed three costly errors and balked in a run as the Royals rallied for a 4–3 victory.

The Royals scored the game-winning run in the top of the ninth when Jim Eisenrich, who singled with two outs, scored from first after Jeff Stone misplayed a fly ball in left field. The miscue negated a strong outing by starter Mike Boddicker, who now had an 0–3 record despite allowing just one earned run and five hits while striking out ten batters in the complete-game loss.

The Orioles actually made the game interesting as they erased a 3–0 deficit by scoring a run in the fifth and two more in the sixth. Fred Lynn started the comeback with his first home run of the year, a shot in the fifth off Royals ace Bret Saberhagen. Billy Ripken's RBI double and Cal Ripken Jr.'s RBI grounder helped tie the game at three after six.

Saberhagen, who retired the first 13 batters he faced, pitched eight strong innings, allowing just three runs (two earned) on seven hits while striking out five to pick up his first victory of the season.

April 15 (0–10): So close, yet so far is the best way to describe the Orioles' 3–2 loss to the Cleveland Indians. Baltimore actually led for five innings before the Indians scored twice in the top of the eighth to cap a late comeback.

Sheets broke out of a season-long slump by connecting on a two-run home run to give the Orioles a 2–1 lead after two. However, late-inning heroics would doom them once again, as outfielder Joe Carter tied the game at two with a one-out homer off starter Scott McGregor.

McGregor would then allow a ground-rule double to designated hitter Ron Kittle before manager Frank Robinson replaced him with reliever Doug Sisk. Sisk gave up a single to third baseman Brook Jacoby, which allowed Kittle to score the eventual game-winning run.

The loss denied McGregor (0–2) a victory despite allowing just three runs on seven hits while striking out six and walking three in 7 1/3 innings. Indians starter Rich Yett beat the Orioles again, as he allowed just two runs on seven hits while striking out four and walking two over seven innings.

Now winless in their first ten games, the Orioles' start represented the worst for a team since the 1920 Detroit Tigers and 1904 Washington Senators each started off losing their first thirteen games.

April 16 (0–11): Of course, the Orioles get nine shutout innings from a starting pitcher and still find a way to lose. That was the case in this game as the Indians held off the Orioles, 1–0, in eleven innings.

First baseman Willie Upshaw drove in the winning run with an

RBI in the top of the 11th to give the Indians all the offense they would need. The eventual game-winning hit came after right fielder Cory Snyder led off the inning with a walk and advanced to second after a passed ball by catcher Carl Nichols. All of this came off reliever Dave Schmidt, who entered the game in the 10th.

Billy Ripken led off the bottom of the 11th with a single off starter Greg Swindell, who was then replaced by reliever Doug Jones. Pinch hitter Jim Traber grounded into a fielder's choice and eventually advanced to third off a double to right field by Eddie Murray.

Jones then retired Cal Ripken Jr. and intentionally walked Larry Sheets before getting Terry Kennedy to strike out looking. Swindell allowed no runs on seven hits, striking out three and walking one on 113 pitches over ten innings.

After this most recent loss, the Orioles had been outscored 66–16 through their first eleven games.

April 17 (0–12): On the plus side, the Orioles ended a 20-inning scoreless drought with a run in the bottom of the third. However, the Indians responded with two runs in the top of the fourth and an insurance run in the top of the seventh to snap a 1–1 tie on the way to a 4–1 victory.

Oswaldo Peraza, who was acquired in the offseason, lost his second straight decision. He allowed three runs on seven hits while striking out two and walking none in just four innings.

The Indians broke open the game in the fourth when Mel Hall delivered an RBI double and Cory Snyder came through with a sacrifice fly off Peraza. Shortstop Jay Bell drove in the Indians' final run on a groundout in the seventh that allowed Hall, who led off the inning with a double, to score.

Indians starter John Farrell became the latest beneficiary of the

Orioles' struggling offense, allowing one earned run on four hits while striking out four and walking three in 8 1/3 innings.

Through twelve games, the Orioles were just 72-for-386 at the plate. This included the heart of Baltimore's lineup, as Cal Ripken Jr., Eddie Murray, and Fred Lynn, were batting .047, .152, and .237, respectively.

April 19 (0–13): While the Orioles finally got some offensive production from key players, their defense and pitching let them down in a 9–5 loss against the host Milwaukee Brewers.

Mark Thurmond lasted just 1 2/3 innings as he allowed five runs (three earned) on five hits and a walk. The Orioles committed four errors in the game, which led to four unearned runs for the Brewers.

With the loss, the Orioles tied the 1904 Washington Senators and 1920 Detroit Tigers for the worst start to the season in MLB history.

"They know they played poorly tonight," Orioles Manager Frank Robinson said to the *Washington Post* after the game. "I don't have to call a meeting and tell them that. We can't tolerate these base-running mistakes and missed signs. What we hadn't done was hit. We did that tonight and it was uplifting, but there were far too many mistakes."

Brewers designated hitter Paul Molitor led the offense by going 3-for-5 with four RBIs. Milwaukee's offensive output, which included scoring three runs in the bottom of the second and fifth, came after the Orioles scored three times in the top of the first.

The three runs represented the most the team had scored in an inning up to that point in the season. Cal Ripken Jr., who entered the game 2-for-43 at the plate, showed signs of life as he hit his first home run, singled, and walked twice (raising his average from .047 to .089).

Mike Boddicker summed up the start to the season while speaking to reporters in the visiting clubhouse after the game. "This is very tough to live through," Boddicker said in a *Washington Post* article. "It's depressing, and at this point all you can do is try to go out and do your job. What the heck, forty or fifty years from now, how many people will remember? Some other team will get started badly, and they'll look it up and find us in the book."

April 20 (0–14): On a cold, dreary Wednesday night, a meager crowd of 7,284 fans at County Stadium witnessed history as the Brewers defeated the Orioles, 8–6. The loss secured the major-league mark for futility to start a season.

After weeks of sleepy bats, the Orioles offense finally came around. However, the team's pitching fell to pieces at the same time. Mike Boddicker had his record fall to 0–4 after he allowed seven runs on seven hits while striking out five and walking four in 4 2/3 innings.

Even so, the Brewers trailed 5–3 heading into the bottom of the fifth. Milwaukee then responded by scoring four times that inning while adding an insurance run in the bottom of the sixth to secure the win.

In the critical fifth inning for the Brewers, center fielder Robin Yount led off with a home run. Five batters later, second baseman Jim Ganter connected on a two-run single to left field to knock Boddicker out of the game. Shortstop Dale Sveum followed and added two more runs on a single to right field off reliever Mark Williamson. The Brewers finished the game with fifteen hits.

April 21 (0–15): A new day brought a new low for the 0–15 Orioles. A six-run bottom of the third was the difference as the Brewers finished the sweep, 7–1.

Scott McGregor felt the brunt of the Brewers offense as he allowed six runs on six hits while striking out one and walking two in 2 2/3 innings. The Brewers recorded six hits, including ones from five-straight batters in the bottom of the third. The inning included a two-run double from left fielder Rob Deer and a two-run homer from catcher Bill Schroeder.

The loss also set the Orioles franchise record for the longest losing streak in team history. The previous mark of fourteen-straight came in 1954, which was the Orioles' first season in Baltimore after moving from St. Louis.

Outfielder Rene Gonzales provided the team with their lone run in the top of the eighth when he hit a two-out single to left field off starter Chris Bosio. The hit allowed Terry Kennedy to score, who reached based on a double two batters earlier.

Bosio improved to 3–1 on the season after allowing one run on eight hits while striking out two in a complete-game victory. The loss by McGregor, whose ERA rose to 8.56, represented his fourteenth defeat in his last seventeen decisions.

The Brewers were now 5–0 against the Orioles in the young season (though 2–7 against the rest of the league). They had also notched 61 hits and 39 runs in those five games, while it took the Orioles until their eleventh game of the season to get over sixty hits and twentieth game to get over forty runs.

April 22 (0–16): Quickly becoming a national story for all the wrong reasons, the Orioles provided more fodder in a 13–1 loss against the host Kansas City Royals.

This game was over almost as soon as it started as the Royals scored nine runs in the first against Mike Morgan, who failed to record an out in his worst outing of the season. Morgan allowed six straight hits before being pulled for reliever Dave Schmidt. Shortstop Kurt Stillwell and center fielder Willie Wilson capped the scoring with back-to-back RBI triples off Schmidt.

The lackluster effort was enough to drive the patience of Orioles manager Frank Robinson, who lashed out at the players after the game. Prior to the loss, Robinson had remained relatively calm and sought to find the positives out of each defeat. The loss represented the longest overall losing streak in the American League since the Detroit Tigers dropped sixteen-straight in 1975.

The Orioles finished with just three hits on the evening. By comparison, Royals outfielder Bo Jackson went 4-for-5 with a home run, three RBIs, and two runs scored. Joe Orsulak drove in the Orioles' lone run of the game when he grounded to first allowing Fred Lynn, who led off the inning with a double, to score in the fifth.

April 23 (0–17): From a blowout the night before to a heart-breaking defeat in the bottom of the ninth, the losses continued to pile up following a 4–3 defeat against the host Royals.

The margin for error continued to be small as the team no longer knew how to react after another loss. Royals shortstop Kurt Stillwell was the latest player to place a dagger in the heart of the Orioles season when he drove in the winning run with a one-out single to center field in the bottom of the ninth off reliever Doug Sisk. Stillwell's hit came two batters after Bo Jackson reached on a triple and Sisk intentionally walked center fielder Thad Bosley in hopes of setting up a double play.

With the loss, the Orioles matched the losing streak of the Atlanta Braves, who lost seventeen-straight in 1977.

"I hate this," said Sisk (0–1) in a postgame interview with the *Washington Post*. "I hate losing. We've got all the excuses, the weather, not getting the breaks, but it's still just losing."

Frank Robinson, who scolded his team for a lack of effort the night before, was ejected for arguing a balk call in the top of the second. This meant he was not in the dugout to watch most of the solid performance from starter Mark Williamson, a converted reliever, who allowed three runs on eight hits while striking out three and walking two over seven innings.

With the game tied at two after four innings, Rene Gonzales gave the Orioles a 3–2 lead with a two-out single to center field off starter Floyd Bannister. The hit allowed Billy Ripken, who doubled the at-bat before, to score from second base. Royals catcher Mike Macfarlane tied the game at three with a one-out RBI single to left field in the bottom of the sixth off Williamson.

To underscore the Orioles' offensive woes, the team had nine regular players batting under .200 at this point of the season: Billy Ripken (.194), Cal Ripken Jr. (.138), Eddie Murray (.179), Ken Gerhart (.154), Tito Landrum (.111), Jeff Stone (.146), Terry Kennedy (.178), Jim Traber (.125), and Wade Rowdon (.111).

April 24 (0–18): For the tenth time in 18 games, the Orioles were held to one or fewer runs, this time being swept by the host Royals, 3–1.

Brett Saberhagen needed just two hours and twenty-four minutes to dispose of the Orioles, going the distance as he allowed a run on six hits while striking out four to pick up the complete-game victory and hand the Orioles their eighteenth consecutive defeat.

The eighteen-game losing streak was the first since the 1975 Detroit Tigers' march with futility. However, this remains the first such streak to begin a season.

The Orioles got only two runners into scoring position the entire game off Saberhagen. The team's lone bright spot came with one out in the ninth when Cal Ripken Jr. ended the shutout bid with a home run to left field. Ripken went 3-for-4, raising his average to a whopping .177.

Mark Thurmond took the loss to drop his record to 0–4. He

allowed three runs on eight hits while striking out three in 5 2/3 innings. The Royals got all the offense they needed in the fifth and sixth: Kurt Stillwell hit a solo home run to left field with two outs in the fifth, while right fielder Danny Tartabull connected on a two-run blast in the sixth off Thurmond.

Tartabull told reporters after the game that playing the Orioles was stressful for the opposing team, as no one wanted to be the first to lose to them.

"When you play the Orioles, you have to play harder than you've ever played in your life," Tartabull said to the *Washington Post.* "You don't want to be the first to lose to them."

April 26 (0–19): Even words of encouragement from President Ronald Reagan were not enough to help the Orioles snap their growing losing streak. This time it was the defending World Series champion and host Minnesota Twins who rallied for a 4–2 victory.

The loss put the Orioles one defeat away from tying the American League record of twenty consecutive losses, set by the 1906 Boston Red Sox and later the Philadelphia Athletics in 1916 (and again in 1943).

Twins starter Frank Viola picked up the win as he allowed two runs on three hits while striking out nine and walking four over seven innings. Once again, Mike Morgan was the tough-luck loser. His record dropped to 0–4 despite allowing just three runs on three hits while striking out two and walking one over six innings.

The Orioles arrived in Minnesota hoping to catch the Twins at just the right time, as they had a 5–11 record entering the series. Leadoff hitter Fred Lynn put the Orioles in great a position just three pitches into the game when he hit a home run off Viola. Cal Ripken Jr. gave Baltimore some breathing room in the top of the third when his double to left field drove in Billy Ripken, who had walked the at-bat before.

However, it took the Twins just five batters in the sixth to rally back and take the lead for good. First baseman Kent Hrbek tied it at two with a two-run home run off Morgan. Morgan then retired the next two batters before right fielder Randy Bush gave the Twins the lead with a home run of his own. Hrbek provided the Twins an insurance run when he led off the bottom of the eighth with another home run, this time off reliever Dave Schmidt.

The Orioles had a chance to rally back in the top of the ninth, as pinch hitter Jeff Stone and Terry Kennedy led off the frame with back-to-back walks off closer Jeff Reardon. However, Reardon settled down after that and got Joe Orsulak to line into a double play and Lynn to fly out in foul territory to seal the team's latest loss.

April 27 (0–20): A fast start and late offensive flurry was not enough for the Orioles, who blew an early lead en route to a 7–6 loss against the Twins.

First baseman Kent Hrbek and catcher Tim Laudner connected on back-to-back home runs, and shortstop Al Newman drove in another on a bunt single in the eighth off reliever Bill Scherrer to help break open a game that had been tied at four.

The loss allowed the Orioles to tie the longest losing streak in American League history and left them only three losses short of tying the all-time losing streak of 23 set by the Philadelphia Phillies in 1961.

Again, the Orioles gave fans a reason for optimism as they scored three runs in the first and another in the second off Twins starter Bert Blyleven. The runs came off an RBI single to left field by Cal Ripken Jr. and a two-run single by Keith Hughes four batters later.

But just like teams had done all season, the Twins rallied back to tie the game at four after scoring two in the bottom of the first and one in the second and fourth off starter Scott McGregor.

McGregor lasted just 3 2/3 innings, allowing four runs on seven hits while striking out one and walking one, extending a winless streak that dated back to May of the previous year.

The Orioles rallied with two outs in the ninth when Ripken Jr. and Eddie Murray came through with back-to-back RBI singles off reliever Keith Atherton. Artherton then settled down and got Fred Lynn to ground out to continue the Orioles' misery.

April 28 (0–21): Mike Boddicker made two mistakes, but that was all the Twins needed to come away with a 4–2 victory in the final game of the series.

The first came in the bottom of the fourth, when Kent Hrbek connected for a two-run home run, while left fielder John Moses came through with a two-out double to right field in the bottom of the sixth.

The loss put the Orioles in the unenviable position of setting the American League record for longest losing streak in a season.

The defeat came after they again jumped out to a 1–0 lead in the first, thanks to a groundout by Eddie Murray that allowed Tito Landrum, who led off the game with a single, to score. The Orioles' only other run came when Twins reliever Mike Mason walked Landrum with the bases loaded, allowing Larry Sheets to score. The game was witnessed by a large media contingent which was usually only reserved for playoff contenders, not ones on such a losing streak.

April 29 (1–21): When Chicago White Sox designated hitter Harold Baines grounded out in the bottom of the ninth, an announced crowd of 14,059 at old Comiskey Park witnessed history: the Orioles had their first victory of the season.

The longest losing streak to ever start an MLB season ended at 21 straight defeats, as the Orioles topped the White Sox 9–0. The Orioles also managed to miss the all-time losing streak by two games.

After so many losses where they would get solid pitching but no hitting, or timely hitting but no pitching or defense, Baltimore finally managed to put a complete game together. Eddie Murray set the tone in the top of the first when he blasted a two-run home run off starter Jack McDowell.

The Orioles then came through with another run in the fifth, followed by four more in the seventh and an additional two in the ninth. Cal Ripken Jr. led the offense by going 4-for-5 with an RBI and three runs scored.

Mark Williamson did the rest as he allowed no runs on three hits and struck out two over six innings to pick up the team's first win of the season. Reliever Dave Schmidt handled the White Sox over the final three innings to pick up the save.

However, even in victory the Orioles were dealt a hardship as Billy Ripken was hit in the head by reliever John Davis during the team's four-run seventh. Ripken was later diagnosed with a concussion but was otherwise OK.

"I'm glad it's over," Williamson said to the *Washington Post* after the game. "We've been trying hard every game, but today we got a few breaks. I thought about this game all last night. Everyone had asked me about the pressure, but I didn't really feel any. What was the pressure?

"The worst we could do is lose one more. I'm relieved, but we have to keep it in perspective. It's not like we just won the seventh game of the World Series. Maybe we won't be so much of a household name now."

THE 1988 ORIOLES: WHERE ARE THEY NOW?

Pitchers:

Don Aase

How acquired: Signed as a free agent to a four-year, $2.4 million deal from the California Angels after the 1984 season.

1988 season: 0–0, 4.05 ERA, 28 strikeouts, 37 walks, 46 2/3 innings pitched in 35 games.

Career stats: 66–60 record with 82 saves and 641 strikeouts and a 3.80 ERA in 448 games for the Boston Red Sox (1977), California Angels (1978–1984), Baltimore Orioles (1985–1988), New York Mets (1989), and Los Angeles Dodgers (1990).

Where are they now? Works as a senior project executive for a waterproofing company in Yorba Linda, California.

Jeff Ballard

How acquired: 27th-round draft choice in 1984 MLB June Amateur Draft out of Stanford.

1988 season: 8–12, 4.40 ERA, 41 strikeouts, 42 walks, 153 1/3 innings pitched in 25 games.

Career stats: 41–53 record with a 4.71 ERA, 244 strikeouts in 773 1/3 innings pitched for the Baltimore Orioles (1987–1991) and Pittsburgh Pirates (1993–1994).

Where are they now? Senior vice president with Ballard Petroleum Holdings in Billings, Montana.

Jose Bautista

How acquired: Rule 5 draft pick from the New York Mets in 1987.

1988 season: 6–15, 4.30 ERA, 76 strikeouts, 45 walks, 171 2/3 innings pitched in 33 games.

Career stats: 32–42 record with a 4.62 ERA, 328 strikeouts in 685 innings pitched for the Baltimore Orioles (1988–1991), Chicago Cubs (1993–1994), San Francisco Giants (1995–1996), Detroit Tigers (1997), and St. Louis Cardinals (1997).

Where are they now? He entered 2019 as the pitching coach of the Kannapolis Intimidators, the Single-A affiliate of the Chicago White Sox.

Mike Boddicker

How acquired: 6th-round of the 1978 MLB June Amateur Draft out of the University of Iowa.

1988 season: 6–12, 3.86 ERA, 100 strikeouts, 51 walks, 147 innings pitched in 21 games for the Orioles; 7–3, 2.63 ERA, 56 strikeouts, 26 walks, 89 innings pitched in 15 games for the Boston Red Sox.

Career stats: 134–116 record with a 3.80 ERA, 1,330 strikeouts in 2,123 2/4 innings pitched for the Baltimore Orioles (1980–1988), Boston Red Sox (1988–1990), Kansas City Royals (1991–1992), and Milwaukee Brewers (1993).

Where are they now? Retired and living in Kansas.

Gordon Dillard
How acquired: 14th round of the 1986 MLB June Amateur Draft out of Oklahoma State University.
1988 season: 0–0, 6.00 ERA, two strikeouts, four walks, three innings pitched in two games.
Career stats: 0–0 record with a 6.43 ERA, 4 walks, four strikeouts in seven innings for the Baltimore Orioles (1988) and Philadelphia Phillies (1989).
Where are they now? Been out of professional baseball since 1991.

John Habyan
How acquired: Third round of the 1982 MLB June Amateur Draft from St. John the Baptist High School (New York).
1988 season: 1–0, 4.30 ERA, four strikeouts, four walks, 14 2/3 innings pitches in seven games.
Career stats: 26–24 record with a 3.85 ERA, 372 strikeouts, 186 walks in 532 innings pitched for the Baltimore Orioles (1985–1988), New York Yankees (1990–1993), Kansas City Royals (1993), St. Louis Cardinals (1994–1995), California Angels (1995), and Colorado Rockies (1996).
Where are they now? Pitching coach at Hofstra University.

Pete Harnisch
How acquired: First round of the 1987 MLB June Amateur Draft out of Fordham University.
1988 season: 0–2, 5.54 ERA, 10 strikeouts, nine walks, 13 innings pitched in two games.
Career stats: 111–103 record with a 3.89 ERA, 1,368 strikeouts, 717 walks in 1,959 innings pitched for the Baltimore Orioles (1988–1990), Houston Astros (1991–1994), New York Mets (1995–1997), Milwaukee Brewers (1997), and Cincinnati Reds (1998–2001)

Where are they now? Special assistant for player development with the Seattle Mariners.

Scott McGregor
How acquired: Traded from the New York Yankees in 1976.
1988 season: 0–3, 8.83 ERA, 10 strikeouts, seven walks, 17 1/3 innings pitched in four games.
Career stats: 138–108 record with a 3.99 ERA, 904 strikeouts, 518 walks, 2,140 2/3 innings pitched for the Baltimore Orioles (1976–1988).
Where are they now? Lives in Baltimore.

Bob Milacki
How acquired: Second round of the 1983 MLB June Draft-Secondary Phase from Yavapai College (Arizona)
1988 season: 2–0, 0.72 ERA, 18 strikeouts, nine walks, 25 innings pitched in three games.
Career stats: 39–47 record with a 4.38 ERA, 387 strikeouts, 85 walks, 795 2/3 innings for the Baltimore Orioles (1988–1992), Cleveland Indians (1993), Kansas City Royals (1994), and Seattle Mariners (1996)
Where are they now? Served as the pitching coach for the Carolina Mudcats, the Single-A affiliate of the Milwaukee Brewers.

Mike Morgan
How acquired: Traded from Seattle Mariners in December 1987.
1988 season: 1–6, 5.43 ERA, 29 strikeouts, 23 walks, 71 1/3 innings pitched in 22 games.
Career stats: 141–186 record with a 4.23 ERA, 1,403 strikeouts, 938 walks in 2,772 1/3 innings for the Oakland Athletics (1978–1979), New York Yankees (1982), Toronto Blue Jays (1983), Seattle

Mariners (1985–1987), Baltimore Orioles (1988), Los Angeles Dodgers (1989–1991), Chicago Cubs (1992–1995, 1998), St. Louis Cardinals (1995–1996), Cincinnati Reds (1996–1997), Minnesota Twins (1998), Texas Rangers (1999), and Arizona Diamondbacks (2000–2002).

Where are they now? Owns World Champion Outfitters in Park City, Utah.

Tom Niedenfuer

How acquired: Traded from Los Angeles Dodgers in May 1987.

1988 season: 3–4, 3.59 ERA, 18 saves, 40 strikeouts, 19 walks, 59 innings pitched in 52 games.

Career stats: 36–46 record, with a 3.29 ERA, 474 strikeouts, 226 walks in 653 innings pitched for the Los Angeles Dodgers (1981–1987), Baltimore Orioles (1987–1988), Seattle Mariners (1989), and St. Louis Cardinals (1990).

Where are they now? Lives in Sarasota, Florida.

Dickie Noles

How acquired: Signed as a free agent in April 1988.

1988 season: 0–2, 24.30 ERA, one strikeout, no walks, 3 1/3 innings in two games.

Career stats: 36–53 with a 4.56 ERA, 455 strikeouts, 338 walks in 860 1/3 innings pitched with the Philadelphia Phillies (1979–1981, 1990) Chicago Cubs (1982–1984, 1987), Texas Rangers (1984–1985), Cleveland Indians (1986), Detroit Tigers (1987), Baltimore Orioles (1988), and New York Yankees (1989).

Where are they now? Works for the Philadelphia Phillies community relations department.

Gregg Olson
How acquired: Drafted in the first round of the 1988 MLB June Amateur Draft out of Auburn University.
1988 season: 1–1, 3.27 ERA, nine strikeouts, ten walks, 11 innings pitched in 11 games.
Career stats: 40–39 with a 3.46 ERA, 217 saves, 588 strikeouts, 330 walks in 672 innings pitched.
Where are they now? Part owner and president of Toolshed Sports.

Oswaldo Peraza
How acquired: Traded from the Toronto Blue Jays in 1987.
1988 season: 5–7, 5.55 ERA, 61 strikeouts, 37 walks, 86 innings in 19 games.
Career stats: 5–7, 5.55 ERA, 61 strikeouts, 37 walks in 86 innings.
Where are they now? Retired from professional baseball after the 1991 season.

Bill Scherrer
How acquired: Signed as a free agent in 1988.
1988 season: 0–1, 8.44 ERA, six strikeouts, five walks, 10 2/3 innings pitched in 12 games.
Career stats: 8–10, 4.08 ERA, 207 strikeouts, 140 walks in 311 1/3 innings pitched for the Cincinnati Reds (1982–1984, 1987), Detroit Tigers (1984–1986), Baltimore Orioles (1988), and Philadelphia Phillies (1988).
Where are they now? Special assistant to Chicago White Sox senior vice president/general manager Rick Hahn.

Curt Schilling
How acquired: Traded from the Boston Red Sox in July 1988.

1988 season: 0–3, 9.92 ERA, four strikeouts, ten walks, 14 2/3 innings pitched in four games.

Career stats: 216–146 with a 3.46 ERA, 3,116 strikeouts, 711 walks in 3,261 innings pitched for the Baltimore Orioles (1988–1990), Houston Astros (1991), Philadelphia Phillies (1992–2000), Arizona Diamondbacks (2000–2003), and Boston Red Sox (2004–2007).

Where are they now? Online radio host with Breitbart.com.

Dave Schmidt

How acquired: Signed as a free agent in 1987.

1988 season: 8–5, 3.40 ERA, 67 strikeouts, 36 walks, 129 2/3 innings in 38 games.

Career stats: 54–55 with a 3.88 ERA, 479 strikeouts, 237 walks in 902 innings pitched for the Texas Rangers (1981–1985), Chicago White Sox (1987–1989), Montreal Expos (1990–1991), and Seattle Mariners (1992).

Where are they now? Spent 2018 as the Orioles' Florida and Latin America pitching coordinator.

Doug Sisk

How acquired: Traded from the New York Mets in 1987.

1988 season: 3–3, 3.72 ERA, 26 strikeouts, 45 walks, 94 1/3 innings pitched in 52 games.

Career stats: 22–20, 3.27 ERA, 195 strikeouts, 267 walks in 523 1/3 innings pitched for the New York Mets (1982–1987), Baltimore Orioles (1988) and Atlanta Braves (1990–91).

Where are they now? Sells fine wine in Tacoma, Washington.

Mark Thurmond

How acquired: Traded from the Detroit Tigers in 1988.

1988 season: 1–8, 4.58 ERA, 29 strikeouts, 27 walks, 74 2/3 innings pitched in 43 games.

Career stats: 40–46 with a 3.69 ERA, 320 strikeouts, 262 walks in 837 2/3 innings pitched for the San Diego Padres (1983–1986), Detroit Tigers (1986–1987), Baltimore Orioles (1988–1989), and San Francisco Giants (1990).

Where are they now? Is vice president for Al Thurmond Insurance Agency in Houston, Texas.

Jay Tibbs

How acquired: Traded from the Montreal Expos in 1988.

1988 season: 4–15, 5.39 ERA, 82 strikeouts, 63 walks, 158 2/3 innings in 30 games.

Career stats: 39–54 with a 4.20 ERA, 448 strikeouts, 319 walks in 862 2/3 innings pitched with the Cincinnati Reds (1984–1985), Montreal Expos (1986–1987), Baltimore Orioles (1988–1989), and Pittsburgh Pirates (1990).

Where are they now? Works in player development with the Southeastern Baseball Management Group.

Mark Williamson

How acquired: Traded from the San Diego Padres in 1986.

1988 season: 5–8, 4.90 ERA, 69 strikeouts, 40 walks, 117 2/3 innings in 37 games.

Career stats: 46–35, 3.86 ERA, 21 saves, 397 strikeouts, 226 walks in 689 2/3 innings pitched with the Baltimore Orioles (1987–1994).

Where are they now? Retired from baseball after the 1994 season.

Catchers

Terry Kennedy
How acquired: Traded from the San Diego Padres in 1986.
1988 season: .226 batting average, three home runs, 16 RBIs, 265 at-bats in 85 games.
Career stats: .264 batting average, 1,313 hits, 113 home runs, 628 RBIs, and 244 doubles for the St. Louis Cardinals (1978–1980), San Diego Padres (1981–1986), Baltimore Orioles (1987–1988), and San Francisco Giants (1990–1991).
Where are they now? A scout for the Chicago Cubs.

Carl Nichols
How acquired: Drafted by the Baltimore Orioles in the fourth round of the 1980 MLB June Amateur Draft.
1988 season: .191 batting average, one RBI, one double, 47 at-bats in 18 games.
Career stats: .204 batting average, 38 hits, 18 RBIs, and eight doubles for the Orioles (1986–1988) and Houston Astros (1990–1991).
Where are they now? Runs the Carl Nichols Baseball Academy.

Mickey Tettleton
How acquired: Signed as a free agent in 1988.
1988 season: .261 batting average, 11 home runs, 37 RBIs, 11 doubles, 283 at-bats in 86 games.
Career stats: .241 batting average, 1,132 hits, 245 home runs, 732 RBIs, 210 doubles, and 711 runs scored for the Oakland Athletics (1984–1987), Baltimore Orioles (1988–1990), Detroit Tigers (1991–1994), and Texas Rangers (1995–1997).
Where are they now? Resides in Norman, Oklahoma.

Infielders

Rene Gonzales

How acquired: Traded from the Montreal Expos in 1986.

1988 season: .215 batting average, two home runs, 15 RBIs, 237 at-bats in 92 games.

Career stats: .239 batting average, 368 hits, 19 home runs, 136 RBIs, 59 doubles, and 185 runs scored for the Montreal Expos (1984–1986), Baltimore Orioles (1987–1990), Toronto Blue Jays (1991), California Angels (1992–1993, 1995), Cleveland Indians (1994), Texas Rangers (1996), and Colorado Rockies (1997).

Where are they now? Living in California.

Eddie Murray

How acquired: Drafted by the Baltimore Orioles in the third round of the 1973 MLB June Amateur Draft from Locke High School (California).

1988 season: .277 batting average, 28 home runs, 84 RBIs, 27 doubles, 75 runs scored, 603 at-bats in 161 games.

Career stats: .287 batting average, 3,255 hits, 504 home runs, 1,917 RBIs, 560 doubles, and 1,627 runs scored for the Baltimore Orioles (1977–1988, 1996), Los Angeles Dodgers (1988–1991, 1997), New York Mets (1992–1993), Cleveland Indians (1994–1996), and Anaheim Angels (1997). Inducted into the National Baseball Hall of Fame in 2003.

Where are they now? Lives in California but makes often visits to Baltimore, where he remains actively involved in numerous charitable organizations.

Billy Ripken

How acquired: Drafted by the Baltimore Orioles in the 11th round of the 1982 MLB June Amateur Draft from Aberdeen High School (Maryland).

1988 season: .207 batting average, two home runs, 34 RBIs, 18 doubles, 52 runs scored, 512 at-bats in 150 games.

Career stats: .247 batting average, 674 hits, 20 home runs, 229 RBIs, 121 doubles, and 287 runs scored for the Baltimore Orioles (1987–1992, 1996), Texas Rangers (1993–1994, 1997), Cleveland Indians (1995), and Detroit Tigers (1998).

Where are they now? Studio analyst for MLB Network and vice president of Ripken Baseball.

Cal Ripken Jr.

How acquired: Drafted by the Baltimore Orioles in the second round of the 1978 MLB June Amateur Draft.

1988 season: .264 batting average, 23 home runs, 81 RBIs, 25 doubles, 87 runs scored, 689 at-bats in 161 games.

Career stats: .276 batting average, 3,184 hits, 431 home runs, 1,695 RBIs, 603 doubles, and 1,647 runs scored for the Baltimore Orioles (1981–2001). Inducted into the National Baseball Hall of Fame in 2007.

Where are they now? President of Ripken Baseball.

Wade Rowdon

How acquired: Traded from the Chicago Cubs in 1988.

1988 season: .100 batting average, one stolen base, 30 at-bats in 20 games.

Career stats: .217 batting average, 34 hits, one home run, 16 RBIs, six doubles and 14 runs scored for the Cincinnati Reds (1984–1986), Chicago Cubs (1987), and Baltimore Orioles (1988).

Where are they now? Retired from baseball after the 1990 season.

Rick Schu

How acquired: Traded from the Philadelphia Phillies in 1988.

1988 season: .256 batting average, four home runs, 20 RBIs, nine doubles, 22 runs scored, 270 at-bats in 89 games.

Career stats: .246 batting average, 386 hits, 41 home runs, 134 RBIs, 67 doubles, and 189 runs scored for the Philadelphia Phillies (1984–1987, 1991), Baltimore Orioles (1988–1989), Detroit Tigers (1989), California Angels (1990), and Montreal Expos (1996).

Where are they now? Assistant hitting coach with the San Francisco Giants.

Jim Traber

How acquired: Drafted by the Orioles in the 21st round of the 1982 MLB June Amateur Draft from Oklahoma State University.

1988 season: .222 batting average, 10 home runs, 45 RBIs, six doubles, 25 runs scored, 352 at-bats in 103 games.

Career stats: .227 batting average, 186 hits, 27 home runs, 117 RBIs, 21 doubles, and 70 runs scored for the Baltimore Orioles (1984–1989).

Where are they now? Sports talk show host in Oklahoma City, Oklahoma.

Craig Worthington

How acquired: First round on the 1985 MLB June Draft-secondary phase from Cerritos College (California).

1988 season: .185 batting average, two home runs, four RBIs, two doubles, 81 at-bats in 26 games.

Career stats: .230 batting average 284 hits, 33 home runs, 144 RBIs, 50 doubles, and 126 runs scored for the Baltimore Orioles (1988–1991), Cleveland Indians (1992), Cincinnati Reds (1995), and Texas Rangers (1995–1996).

Where are they now? Retired from professional baseball in 2000.

Outfielders

Brady Anderson

How acquired: Traded from the Boston Red Sox in July 1988.

1988 season: .212 batting average, one home run, 21 RBIs, 13 doubles, four triples, ten stolen bases, 31 runs scored, 325 at-bats in 94 games.

Career stats: .256 batting average, 1,661 hits, 210 home runs, 761 RBIs, 338 doubles, 67 triples, 315 stolen bases, and 1,062 runs scored for the Boston Red Sox (1988), Baltimore Orioles (1988–2001), and Cleveland Indians (2002).

Where are they now? Vice president of baseball operations for the Baltimore Orioles.

Butch Davis

How acquired: Signed as a free agent in 1988.

1988 season: .240 batting average, two runs scored, 25 at-bats in 13 games.

Career stats: .243 batting average, 110 hits, seven home runs, 50 RBIs, 21 doubles, and 56 runs scored for the Kansas City Royals (1983–1984), Pittsburgh Pirates (1987), Baltimore Orioles (1988–1989), Los Angeles Dodgers (1991), and Texas Rangers (1993–1994).

Where are they now? Lives in Garner, North Carolina. Worked as coach in minor and major leagues from 1997 to 2016.

Jim Dwyer

How acquired: Signed as a free agent in 1980.

1988 season: .255 batting average, two home runs, 18 RBIs, nine runs scored, 53 at-bats in 35 games.

Career stats: .260 batting average, 719 hits, 77 home runs, 349 RBIs, 115 doubles, and 409 runs scored for the St. Louis Cardinals

(1973–1975, 1977–1978), Montreal Expos (1975–1976), New York Mets (1976), San Francisco Giants (1978), Boston Red Sox (1979–1980), Baltimore Orioles (1981–1988), and Minnesota Twins (1988–1990).

Where are they now? Retired and living in Cape Coral, Florida, after a long minor league managerial career.

Ken Gerhart

How acquired: Drafted by the Baltimore Orioles in the fifth round of the 1982 MLB June Amateur Draft from Middle Tennessee State.

1988 season: .195 batting average, nine home runs, 23 RBIs, 10 doubles, seven stolen bases, 27 runs scored, 262 at-bats in 103 games.

Career stats: .221 batting average, 136 hits, 24 home runs, 64 RBIs, 16 stolen bases, and 72 runs scored for the Baltimore Orioles (1986–1988).

Where are they now? Lives in Murfreesboro, Tennessee.

Keith Hughes

How acquired: Traded from the Philadelphia Phillies in 1988.

1988 season: .194 batting average, two home runs, 14 RBIs, four doubles, 10 runs scored, 108 at-bats in 41 games.

Career stats: .204 batting average, 41 hits, two home runs, 24 RBIs, six doubles, and 18 runs scored for the New York Yankees (1987), Philadelphia Phillies (1987), Baltimore Orioles (1988), New York Mets (1990), and Cincinnati Reds (1993).

Where are they now? Retired from professional baseball in 1995.

Tito Landrum

How acquired: Signed as a free agent in 1988.

1988 season: .125 batting average, two RBIs, one triple, 24 at-bats in 13 games.

Career stats: .249 batting average, 248 hits, 13 home runs, 40 doubles, and 120 runs scored for the St. Louis Cardinals (1980–1982, 1984–1987) Baltimore Orioles (1983, 1988), and Los Angeles Dodgers (1987).

Where are they now? A physical therapist in New York City.

Fred Lynn

How acquired: Signed as a free agent in 1984.

1988 season: .246 batting average, 25 home runs, 56 RBIs, 14 doubles, 46 runs scored, 391 at-bats in 114 games.

Career stats: .283 batting average, 1,960 hits, 306 home runs, 388 doubles, 1,111 RBIs, and 1,063 runs scored for the Boston Red Sox (1974–1980), California Angels (1981–1984), Baltimore Orioles (1985–1988), Detroit Tigers (1988–1989), and San Diego Padres (1990).

Where are they now? Retired and living in California.

Joe Orsulak

How acquired: Traded from the Pittsburgh Pirates in 1987.

1988 season: .288 batting average, eight home runs, 27 RBIs, nine stolen bases, 48 runs scored, 379 at-bats in 125 games.

Career stats: .273 batting average, 1,173 hits, 57 home runs, 405 RBIs, 186 doubles, 93 stolen bases, and 559 runs scored for the Pittsburgh Pirates (1983–1986), Baltimore Orioles 1988–1992), New York Mets (1993–1995), Florida Marlins (1996), and Montreal Expos (1997).

Where are they now? Living in Maryland.

Larry Sheets

How acquired: Drafted in the second round of the 1978 MLB June Amateur Draft from Lee High School in Virginia.

1988 season: .230 batting average, 10 home runs, 47 RBIs, 19 doubles, 38 runs scored, 452 at-bats in 136 games.

Career stats: .266 batting average, 607 hits, 94 home runs, 339 RBIs, 98 doubles, and 273 runs scored for the Baltimore Orioles (1984–1989), Detroit Tigers (1990), and Seattle Mariners (1993).

Where are they now? Head baseball coach at Gilman School, a private school in Baltimore, Maryland.

Pete Stanicek

How acquired: Drafted in the ninth round of the 1985 MLB June Amateur Draft from Stanford University.

1988 season: .230 batting average, four home runs, 17 RBIs, seven doubles, 12 stolen bases, 29 runs scored, 261 at-bats in 83 games.

Career stats: .243 batting average, four home runs, 26 RBIs, ten doubles, 20 stolen bases, and 38 runs scored for the Baltimore Orioles (1987–1988).

Where are they now? Chief of staff legal & CASSIP Ops at Health Care Service Corporation, Blue Cross Blue Shield.

Jeff Stone

How acquired: Traded from the Philadelphia Phillies in 1988.

1988 season: .164 batting average, one double, four stolen bases, four runs scored, 61 at-bats in 26 games.

Career stats: .277 batting average, 261 hits, 11 home runs, 72 RBIs, 23 doubles, 18 triples, 75 stolen bases, and 129 runs scored for the Philadelphia Phillies (1983–1987), Baltimore Orioles (1988), Texas Rangers (1989), and Boston Red Sox (1989–1990).

Where are they now? Last played professional baseball in 1992.

Manager

Cal Ripken Sr.

How acquired: Named manager in 1987.

1988 season: Was fired after losing first six games of the 1988 season.

Career stats: 68–101 career managerial record.

Where are they now? Died on March 25, 1999, of lung cancer. He was sixty-three years old.

Frank Robinson

How acquired: Named manager seven games into the 1988 season.

1988 season: 54–101 record.

Career stats: 1,065–1,176 record with the Cleveland Indians (1975–1977), San Francisco Giants (1981–1984), Baltimore Orioles (1988–1991), Montreal Expos (2002–2004), and Washington Nationals (2005–2006).

Where are they now? Was the Senior Advisor to MLB commissioner and the honorary president of the American League until his passing in February of 2019, at the age of eighty-three.

Coaches

Don Buford (bench)

How acquired: Joined staff in 1988.

Playing career stats: .264 batting average, 93 home runs, 418 RBIs, 718 runs scored, and 200 stolen bases for Chicago White Sox (1963–1967) and Baltimore Orioles (1968–1972). Also served as minor league manager, assistant farm director, and farm director for Orioles.

Where are they now? Founded Educational Sports Institute in Watts, California.

Terry Crowley (hitting)

How acquired: Named Orioles hitting coach in 1985.

Playing career stats: .250 batting average, 379 hits, 42 home runs, and 229 RBIs for the Baltimore Orioles (1969–1973, 1976–1982), Cincinnati Reds (1974–1975), Atlanta Braves (1976), and Montreal Expos (1983). Served as Orioles hitting coach from 1985–1988 and 1999–2010. Held the same title for the Minnesota Twins from 1991–1998.

Where are they now? Retired.

John Hart (third base)

How acquired: Joined organization as minor league manager in 1982. Named third base coach in 1988.

Career stats: Served as general manager for the Cleveland Indians (1991–2001) and Texas Rangers (2002–2005). Served as senior advisor to Texas Rangers from 2005 to 2013, and for the Atlanta Braves in 2014. Served as president of baseball operations for the Atlanta Braves from 2014–2017.

Where are they now? Resigned from the Atlanta Braves on November 17, 2017.

Elrod Hendricks (bullpen)

How acquired: Acquired as a player in the 1967 Rule 5 Draft from the California Angels.

Playing career stats: 220 batting average, 415 hits, 62 home runs, 230 RBIs, 66 doubles, and 205 runs for the Baltimore Orioles (1968–1972, 1973–1976, 1978–1979), Chicago Cubs (1973), and New York Yankees (1976–1977). Served as bullpen coach from 1977–2005.

Where are they now? Died of a heart attack on December 21, 2005. He was sixty-four years old.

Minnie Mendoza (first base)

How acquired: Named first base coach in 1988.

Playing career stats: .188 batting average with 20 RBIs for the Minnesota Twins (1970). Also served as a minor league manager and roving minor league instructor for the Baltimore Orioles.

Where are they now? Advisor in the Cleveland Indians organization.

Herm Starrette (pitching)

How acquired: Signed by the Orioles as an amateur free agent in 1958. Named Orioles pitching coach in 1988.

Playing career stats: 1–1 record with a 2.54 ERA in 46 innings pitched for Orioles from 1963–1965. Would spend twenty-eight years as a pitching coach, bullpen coach, minor league instructor, coordinator of instruction, and farm system director with the Atlanta Braves, Baltimore Orioles, San Francisco Giants, Philadelphia Phillies, Milwaukee Brewers, Chicago Cubs, Montreal Expos, and Boston Red Sox. He was the pitching coach of the 1980 World Series champion Phillies.

Where are they now? He died on June 2, 2017. He was eighty years old.

Front office

Edward Bennett Williams (Owner)

How acquired: Purchased the Baltimore Orioles in 1980.

Career stats: A trial attorney by trade, Williams at one point owned the Orioles and had a stake in the Washington Redskins. Williams's stake in the franchises was still in place in 1983, when the Orioles won the World Series and the Redskins won the Super Bowl.

Where are they now? Died of cancer on August 13, 1988. He was sixty-eight years old.

Roland Hemond (General Manager)

How acquired: Named general manager of the Baltimore Orioles prior to the 1988 season.

Career stats: Hemond served as general manager for the Chicago White Sox from 1970 to 1985, and for the Orioles from 1988 to 1995. He later served as senior executive vice president for the Arizona Diamondbacks from 1996 to 2000 and as an executive adviser for the White Sox from 2001 to 2007.

Where are they now? He is retired.

ACKNOWLEDGEMENTS

I would like to thank the following people for helping me make this project possible:

Greg Bader: Thank you for offering the support of this project from the Orioles.

Bill Stetka: Appreciate the help connecting me with former players with the Orioles.

John Maroon: Thanks for assisting in making key interviews possible.

Keith Mills and Scott Garceau: Two sports broadcast figures in Baltimore whose knowledge and insight helped so much.

Cal Ripken Jr.: I appreciate the unique perspective you offered playing on both a World Series team and one that had the worst start to a season in baseball history.

Others I would like to thank include:

Brooks Robinson

Dave Johnson

Jeff Ballard

Mike Devereaux

Gregg Olson

Fred Lynn

Joe Orsulak

Ron Shapiro

Roy Firestone

Jose Bautista

Dave Schmidt

John Habyan

Michael Olesker

Harold Baines

Michael Gibbons